P9-DWJ-440

a little taste of...

india

a little taste of...

india

Recipes by Priya Wickramasinghe
and Carol Selva Rajah
Photography by Jason Lowe (location)
and Alan Benson (recipes)
Additional text by Kay Halsey

MURDOCH
BOOKS

contents

SPECIAL FEATURES

a little taste...

Indian food is one of the world's most popular cuisines, but outside of India the blur of chilli heat makes many dishes taste the same, the subtleties of the spicing obscured by the liberal use of curry and chilli powders. Indian cooking can be spicy, but it is not universally so, and many dishes don't contain any chillies at all. Instead, Indian food is all about its inspired use of wonderful spices and herbs. Every dish is created from a unique blend of flavourings, and the complex interaction of the ingredients in this *masala*, spice mix, is what gives Indian food its flavour, colour, heat and fantastic aroma.

Most Indian restaurant food is a rich interpretation of northern cooking, evolved by the subcontinent's most successful restaurateurs, the Punjabis and Bangladeshis. But the everyday food eaten in India is incredibly diverse across both regions and communities. A commercial kitchen may be called upon to produce as many as 10 or more menus catering for different religious and social groups, while at the very least meals are divided into vegetable and non-vegetable. The Hindu belief that the purity of mind and body can be guaranteed by a wholesome diet has created a huge vegetarian population, especially in Gujarat and the South, even though the eating of meat, except for beef, is not taboo in Hinduism. Many vegetarian Buddhists and Jains also abstain from the strong tastes of onion and garlic, while the Muslim population will not touch pork. Other communities have diets so restricted that it is hard to eat outside the home at all. '*Dal and roti*' (a stew-like dish of pulses with bread), a meal acceptable to all, has virtually become the national dish and Indian vegetarian cooking one of the most creative and delicious of all cuisines.

An Indian meal is generally much more complex in composition than its Western counterpart. Usually there will be one meat and one vegetable dish (or two vegetarian dishes), a pulse, some hot breads or rice, a pot of curds, yoghurt relish, or a fresh chutney or small salad, and often a pickle. All these must be in perfect balance, the cook ensuring that not all the dishes are spicy hot and that there is a contrast of colours, flavours and textures. There will be perhaps one 'wet' and one 'dry' curry, and the relishes are chosen to complement the meal. To follow, there is rarely dessert, usually just some sliced fruit.

Unlike many countries where communal dishes are placed on the table for everyone to dig in, Indian food is more likely to be served up individually, a spoonful of each dish placed on a *thali*, an Indian platter, and eaten with great dexterity using just the fingertips of the right hand. The rice is deftly blended with the curry into bite-size balls, or wrapped in a piece of torn *roti*, bread, the lack of cutlery adding an agreeably tactile element to eating.

a little taste of...

Tiffin was the food of colonial India, a light lunch that was part British nursery food and part spicy Indian titbits: leftover roasts, breaded cutlets, pickles, salads, jellies and ice-cream, the Sunday 'curry tiffin' a specialty of clubs and hotels all over India. Its origins may have been European, but nowadays tiffin is most definitely Indian, the word adopted for the multitude of snacks that are a national passion. For the Indians, a meal must involve real sustenance, a plate of rice or some breads. Anything else is considered just a snack, and no day is complete without a cup of *masala chai* and a samosa. The Indians tend to eat dinner late, so tiffin bridges the gap after lunch, workers clustering at sunset around roadside stalls, chatting and enjoying crispy vegetable *bhajis* or tasty minced meat kebabs. In the South, tiffin is almost always vegetarian, and as likely to be breakfast as a late afternoon snack. Thin rice *dosas* stuffed with spicy potato are a favourite, and *vadai*, lentil doughnuts, or *idlis*, soft rice cakes, are served alongside a bowl of coconut and tamarind chutney.

...tiffin

singharas

PASTRY
250 g (2 cups) maida or plain
  (all-purpose) flour
2 tablespoons ghee

MEAT FILLING
4 ripe tomatoes
2 tablespoons ghee or oil
2 cinnamon sticks
6 cloves
1 cardamom pod
3 green chillies, chopped

1 large onion, finely chopped
3–4 curry leaves
4 garlic cloves, crushed
1 teaspoon ground turmeric
5 cm (2 in) piece of ginger, grated
500 g (1 lb 2 oz) minced (ground) lamb
150 g (1 cup) peas
1 teaspoon garam masala (page 251)

oil, for deep-frying

Makes 2

To make the pastry, sift the maida and a pinch of salt into a bowl. Rub in the ghee until the mixture resembles breadcrumbs. Add 125 ml (½ cup) warm water, a little at a time, to make a pliable dough. Turn out onto a floured surface and knead for 5 minutes, or until the dough is smooth. Cover and set aside for 30 minutes. Don't refrigerate or the ghee will harden.

To make the meat filling, score a cross in the top of each tomato. Plunge into boiling water for 20 seconds, drain and peel away from the cross, then roughly chop, discarding the cores and seeds and reserving any juices. Heat the ghee in a *karhai* or saucepan over low heat and fry the cinnamon, cloves, cardamom and chilli. Add the onion, curry leaves, garlic, turmeric and ginger and fry for 5 minutes, or until the onion is brown. Add the lamb, fry until brown, then add the tomato and cover with a tight lid. Cook gently, stirring occasionally until the lamb is tender. Add the peas, cover and cook for 5 minutes. If there is any liquid left, turn up the heat and let it evaporate. Remove the whole spices. Season with salt, to taste, and sprinkle with garam masala.

Divide the dough into 12 portions, roll out each to a 12 cm (5 in) circle, then cut each circle in half. Take one piece and form a hollow cone by folding the dough in half and sealing the two edges of the cut side together. (Wet one edge and make a small overlap.) Fill to three-quarters full with filling. Seal the top edges, then pinch to give a fluted finish. Repeat with the remaining dough.

Fill a *karhai* or saucepan to one-third full with oil and heat to 180°C (350°F/ Gas 4), or until a cube of bread browns in 15 seconds. Fry the singharas until browned. Drain on a wire rack and keep them warm in a low oven.

**250 g (2 cups) maida or plain
  (all-purpose) flour**
1 teaspoon salt
1 teaspoon kalonji (nigella seeds)
1 tablespoon ghee
oil, for deep-frying

Makes 60

Sift the maida and salt into a bowl and add the kalonji. Rub in the ghee until the mixture resembles breadcrumbs. Add about 150 ml (½ cup) water, a little at a time, to make a pliable dough. Turn the dough out onto a floured surface and knead for 5 minutes, or until smooth, then cover and rest it for 10 minutes. Don't refrigerate or the ghee will harden.

Divide the dough into two portions and roll out each portion until about 3 mm (⅛ in) thick. Cut into 1 cm (½ in) wide strips, then into diamonds about 3 cm (1 in) long, by making diagonal cuts along the strips. Prick the diamonds with a fork.

Fill a *karhai* or heavy-based saucepan to one-third full with oil and heat to about 170°C (325°F/Gas 3), or until a cube of bread browns in 20 seconds when dropped in the oil. Fry the nimki in batches until light golden and crisp. Drain on paper towels. Serve with mint and coriander chutney (page 48).

nimki

chaat

Chaat literally means 'finger-licking good' in Hindi, and there couldn't be a better name for these tasty little snacks. The most famous *chaats* are found on the beaches of Mumbai, where stallholders serve up seaside snacks in disposable leaf bowls or tiny metal trays. These include Mumbai's favourite, *bhel puri*, a zesty mix of puffed rice, potato and green mango held together with a tart tamarind chutney. *Aloo chaat* is a tangy Indian potato salad, and *chole chaat*, spicy chickpeas, is at its most delicious served over fried potato cakes. *Pani puris*, or *gol gappas*, hold a special place in Indian affections, tingling mouthfuls of potato, chickpeas and tamarind water stuffed into fried bread puffs.

As a snack, chaats don't have to be filling or nutritionally balanced. Instead they are meant to titillate your tastebuds and arouse the appetite, incorporating diverse flavours from sour chutneys, sweet fruit and hot chillies to cooling yoghurt. They also all share a distinctive final garnish of black salt, lemon, and a pinch of *chaat masala*, a sour, salty mix flavoured with *amchoor*, green mango powder.

chucumber

1 red onion, finely chopped
2 small cucumbers, about 200 g (7 oz),
   finely chopped
100 g (4 oz) ripe tomatoes, finely chopped
3 tablespoons finely chopped coriander
   (cilantro)
1 red chilli, finely chopped
1 green chilli, finely chopped
1½ tablespoons lemon juice
1 teaspoon oil
125 g (¾ cup) unroasted peanuts,
   roughly chopped
1 teaspoon salt
½ teaspoon ground black pepper
1½ teaspoons chaat masala (page 251)

Serves 4

Stir together in a bowl the onion, cucumber, tomato, coriander, chillies and lemon juice.

Heat the oil in a *karhai* or heavy-based frying pan over high heat, add the peanuts and salt and fry for 1 minute. Sprinkle with the pepper and chaat masala and stir. Fry for 2 minutes. Remove from the heat and add to the onion mixture. Season with more salt, to taste, just before serving. The seasoning is added at the end to prevent the ingredients from releasing too much juice before serving.

Serve in small bowls. Chucumber can be eaten with a spoon or scooped up in pieces of roti (saag roti, page 146) or poppadoms.

1 kg (2 lb 4 oz) lamb cutlets
3/4 teaspoon cumin seeds
1 teaspoon coriander seeds
3/4 teaspoon black peppercorns
500 ml (2 cups) milk
2 cinnamon sticks
10 cardamom seeds
10 cloves
2 cm (3/4 in) piece of ginger, grated
2 onions, finely chopped
75 g (2/3 cup) besan flour
2 teaspoons chilli powder
125 ml (1/2 cup) thick plain yoghurt
   or recipe page 250
oil, for deep-frying
lime quarters

Serves 6

Trim the lamb of any fat and scrape the bone ends clean. Place a small frying pan over low heat and dry-roast the cumin seeds until aromatic. Remove them and dry-roast the coriander seeds. Crush the coriander and cumin seeds with the peppercorns in a spice grinder or use a mortar and pestle. Transfer to a large, heavy-based saucepan and add the milk, cinnamon, cardamom, cloves, ginger and onion. Bring to the boil over medium heat, then add the chops to the pan and return to the boil. Reduce the heat and simmer for 30 minutes, or until the meat is tender and very little liquid remains. Remove the cutlets and drain them.

Whisk the besan flour and chilli powder into the yoghurt with 60 ml (1/2 cup) water, to make a batter.

Fill a *karhai* or heavy-based saucepan to one-third full of oil and heat to 180°C (350°F/Gas 4), or until a cube of bread fries brown in 15 seconds when dropped in the oil. Dip the cutlets in the batter, shake off any excess, then fry them in batches in the hot oil until they are crisp. Drain on paper towels and keep them warm. Serve sprinkled with a little lime juice and salt, to taste.

kashmiri lamb cutlets

prawn pakoras

600 g (1 lb 5 oz) prawns (shrimp)
50 g (½ cup) besan (chickpea) flour
1 large red onion, finely chopped
1 teaspoon dried pomegranate seeds
4 green chillies, seeded and finely chopped
2 tablespoons finely chopped coriander
   (cilantro) leaves
pinch of bicarbonate of soda
ghee or oil, for deep-frying

Makes 30

Peel and devein the prawns, then cut into small pieces. Put the besan flour in a bowl and add 2 tablespoons of water, or enough to make a thick batter, mixing with a fork to beat out any lumps. Add the remaining ingredients, except the oil, to the batter. Season with salt and mix well.

Fill a *karhai* or heavy-based saucepan to one-third full with ghee and heat to 180°C (350°F/Gas 4), or until a cube of bread browns in 15 seconds. Drop 1 heaped teaspoon of batter at a time into the ghee and deep-fry in batches of six or eight pakoras until they are brown all over. Remove and drain on paper towels. Serve hot.

325 g (2²/₃ cups) maida or plain
  (all-purpose) flour
125 g (1 cup) fine semolina
oil, for deep-frying

Makes 12 large or 35 crisps

Mix the maida and semolina with 100 ml (½ cup) water into a dough and knead well until firm. If necessary, add more flour to make it a very firm dough. Cover and leave for 1 hour.

To make puri, knead the dough again, then divide into 12 balls. Roll each dough ball out to 1 mm (¹/₁₂ in) thick (not too thin), making a circle of about 10 cm (4 in) in diameter.

Fill a *karhai* or heavy-based saucepan to one-third full with oil and heat to 180°C (350°F/Gas 4). Test the temperature by putting a small piece of the dough into the oil. If the dough rises to the surface in a couple of seconds, the oil is ready. Put a puri into the hot oil, then about 5 seconds after it rises to the surface, gently push it down, using the back of a spoon, to keep it submerged in the hot oil until it puffs up; this will also take about 5 seconds. Turn over and cook until the other side is lightly browned. Remove from the oil and drain on a wire rack. This frying process should take 15–20 seconds for each puri. Continue until all the puris are cooked.

To make puri crisps, roll out the kneaded dough to 1 mm (¹/₁₂ in) thick (not too thin), cut out circles with a 4 cm (1½ in) diameter with a pastry cutter and set them aside on a tray.

Fill a *karhai* or heavy-based saucepan to one-third full with oil and heat until a small ball of dough rises to the surface in a few seconds. Deep-fry the puri crisps in batches until golden and puffed. Drain the puris on paper towels. If you have any remaining pastry, cut it into pieces and deep-fry to make irregular-shaped crisps.

puris

bhel puri

MINT CHUTNEY
50 g (1²/₃ cups) coriander (cilantro) leaves
50 g (2½ cups) mint leaves
6 garlic cloves, chopped
3 red chillies, chopped
½ red onion, chopped
3 tablespoons lemon juice

TAMARIND CHUTNEY
60 g (2 oz) fennel seeds
450 ml (1½ cups) tamarind purée
    (page 250)
100 g (4 oz) ginger, sliced
300 g (1²/₃ cups) jaggery or soft
    brown sugar
1 teaspoon chilli powder
1 tablespoon ground cumin

1 tablespoon chaat masala (page 251)
1 teaspoon black salt

3 potatoes
1 tomato
120 g (4 oz) puffed rice
60 g (2 oz) sev noodles
1 green unripe mango, sliced into slivers
1 onion, finely chopped
4 tablespoons finely chopped coriander
    (cilantro) or mint leaves
1 teaspoon chaat masala (page 251)
12 crushed puri crisps (page 24)

coriander (cilantro) leaves

Serves 6

To make the mint chutney, blend the ingredients in a food processor or use a mortar and pestle. Transfer to a saucepan and bring to the boil. Remove from the heat, leave to cool, then season with salt. This chutney can't be stored.

To make the tamarind chutney, place a frying pan over low heat and dry-roast the fennel seeds until aromatic. Mix together the tamarind, ginger and sugar with 250 ml (1 cup) water in a saucepan. Cook over low heat until the tamarind blends into the mixture and the sugar dissolves. Strain the ginger, then cook the mixture to a thick pulp. Add the fennel seeds, chilli powder, cumin, chaat masala and black salt. Season with salt and reduce, stirring occasionally, over medium heat until thickened to a dropping consistency. Leave to cool.

To make the bhel puri, cook the potatoes in boiling water for 10 minutes or until tender, then cut into cubes. Score a cross in the top of the tomato. Plunge into boiling water for 20 seconds, then drain and peel. Chop the tomato, discarding the core and seeds and reserving any juices. Put the puffed rice, noodles, mango, onion, chopped coriander, chaat masala and puri crisps in a bowl and mix them together. Stir in a little of each chutney. Vary the amounts of chutney depending on the flavour you want to achieve (the tamarind is tart and the mint is hot). Serve in bowls and garnish with coriander leaves. You can store this chutney in a jar in the fridge where it will keep for several weeks.

250 g (9 oz) chickpeas
1 large onion, roughly chopped
2 garlic cloves, roughly chopped
5 cm (2 in) piece of ginger, roughly
   chopped
1 green chilli, chopped
160 ml (²⁄₃ cup) oil
1 tablespoon ground cumin
1 tablespoon ground coriander (cilantro)
1 teaspoon chilli powder
pinch of asafoetida
2 tablespoons thick plain yoghurt
   or recipe page 250
2¹⁄₄ tablespoons garam masala (page 251)

2 teaspoons tamarind purée (page 250)
¹⁄₂ lemon
3 green chillies, extra
¹⁄₄ teaspoon ground black pepper
3 teaspoons salt
2 teaspoons chaat masala (page 251)
¹⁄₂ red onion, sliced into thin rings
2 cm (³⁄₄ in) piece of ginger, cut into thin
   strips
coriander (cilantro) leaves, roughly
   chopped (optional)

Serves 6

Soak the chickpeas overnight in 2 litres (8 cups) of water. Drain, then put the chickpeas in a large saucepan with another 2 litres (8 cups) water. Bring to the boil, spooning off any scum from the surface, then simmer over low heat for 1–1¹⁄₂ hours, until soft. It is important the chickpeas are soft at this stage as they won't soften once the sauce has been added. Drain the chickpeas, reserving the cooking liquid.

Bend the onion, garlic, ginger and chopped chilli to a paste in a food processor or very finely chop them together with a knife.

Heat the oil in a heavy-based saucepan over medium heat and fry the onion mixture until golden brown. Add the cumin, coriander, chilli powder and asafoetida, then stir for 1 minute. Add the yoghurt and stir for another minute. Stir in 2 tablespoons of the garam masala and pour in 1.25 litres (4¹⁄₂ cups) of the reserved cooking liquid, a little at a time, stirring after each addition. Bring to the boil, then reduce the heat to simmering point.

Add the tamarind purée, lemon, whole chillies, chickpeas, pepper and the salt. Partially cover the pan, simmer for 30 minutes, then remove the lemon. Cook the sauce for another 30 minutes, or until all the liquid has reduced, leaving the softened chickpeas coated in a rich dark brown sauce.

Add the chaat masala and remaining garam masala and stir in the raw onion rings, ginger and coriander leaves, if using.

chana masala

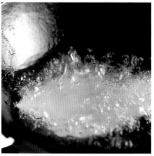

kachoris

FILLING
100 g (4 oz) urad dal
1½ tablespoons oil
1 teaspoon cumin seeds
¼ teaspoon ground turmeric
¼ teaspoon asafoetida
3 green chillies, finely chopped (optional)
2 cm (¾ in) piece of ginger, grated

DOUGH
200 g (1⅓ cups) atta (chapati) flour, or
   100 g (¾ cup) wholemeal flour, mixed
   with 100 g (1 cup) maida or plain
   (all-purpose) flour
1 teaspoon kalonji (nigella seeds)
2 teaspoons oil or ghee

oil, for deep-frying

Makes 20

To make the filling, begin by soaking the urad dal in 500 ml (2 cups) of cold water for 2 hours. Drain and chop in a food processor for a few seconds to form a coarse paste. If you don't have a food processor, grind the dal in a mortar and pestle. Heat the oil over medium heat in a saucepan, add the cumin seeds, then cover and allow the seeds to pop. Add the turmeric, asafoetida, chilli and ginger and stir until well mixed. Add the dal paste and 125 ml (½ cup) water and cook over low heat, stirring until the liquid has evaporated. Add salt, to taste. Spread on a plate and leave until cold.

To make the dough, sift the atta and a little salt into a bowl and add the kalonji. Rub in the oil until the mixture resembles breadcrumbs. Add 140–170 ml (½–⅔ cup) warm water, a little at a time, to make a pliable dough. Turn out onto a floured surface and knead for 5 minutes, or until the dough is smooth. Cover and set aside for 15 minutes. Don't refrigerate or the oil will harden.

Divide the dough into 20 balls. Roll one out on a floured surface to resemble a thin pancake 8–10 cm (3–4 in) in diameter. Place 1 heaped teaspoon of the dal mixture in the centre, then fold over the dough to form into a semicircle. Pinch the edges together to seal. Gently roll out on a floured surface; try to retain the semicircular shape. Repeat to use all the dough and filling.

Fill a *karhai* or heavy-based saucepan to one-third full with oil and heat to 180°C (350°F/Gas 4), or until a cube of bread fries brown in 15 seconds when dropped in the oil. Lower a kachori into the oil and, when it rises to the surface, gently push it down using the back of a spoon, to keep it submerged until it puffs up. Turn it over and cook until the other side is lightly browned. Drain on a wire rack and keep the kachori warm while you cook the rest.

yoghurt... India's sacred cows may not be used for meat, but they make perhaps an even more invaluable contribution to the Indian diet with their milk. The Indians don't actually drink much milk; instead, they turn it into an amazing array of dairy products, from *dahi,* yoghurt, to cheese and sweets. More easily digestible than milk, these products can also be stored for longer and provide essential protein to what is, for many, a meat-free diet.

Many Indian households prepare their own yoghurt from fresh milk. More than just milk that has been left to go sour, the milk needs bacteria added to

ferment it, breaking down its sugars into the lactic acid that gives yoghurt its characteristically sour taste. This basic yoghurt, known as curds in India, is an essential part of every vegetarian meal. A tiny clay or metal pot will hold a spoonful of plain or a fresh fruit or vegetable *raita*, both effective ways of neutralizing the heat of chilli-infused dishes. Yoghurt is also used extensively in the Indian kitchen, the lactic acid acting as a meat tenderizer in spice and herb marinades, the yoghurt's creamy texture a way of thickening sauces.

One of the most delicious uses of curds is to make *lassi*, an icy cold yoghurt drink. Lassis are served sweet or salty, and are made by diluting yoghurt with a little water, whisking until frothy, then serving over ice. High-quality yoghurt is essential, as even diluted with water it needs to retain its slightly sour edge and thick, creamy consistency. The sweet lassi is flavoured with sugar, rosewater, scented lime or, increasingly, ripe tropical fruit such as mangoes. The salty version is served plain or with a little chopped fresh mint and is the perfect partner for a hot curry. Being India, there are also surprisingly refreshing spicy versions, the yoghurt drink dusted with a pinch of roasted cumin seeds or black pepper at one of the North's countless roadside lassi stalls, or mixed with a wet paste of green chilli, ginger, fresh coriander and garlic in the South.

MARINADE
3 teaspoons coriander (cilantro) seeds
2 teaspoons cumin seeds
4 cm (1½ in) piece of cinnamon stick
1 teaspoon cardamom seeds
1 onion, roughly chopped
6–8 garlic cloves, roughly chopped
2.5 cm (1 in) piece of ginger,
    roughly chopped
½ teaspoon ground cloves
½ teaspoon cayenne pepper
3 tablespoons oil
1 tablespoon tomato purée
3 tablespoons clear vinegar
1 teaspoon salt

600 g (1 lb 5 oz) skinless chicken breast
    fillets, cut into 1 cm (½ in) strips

Serves 6

To make the marinade, place a frying pan over low heat and dry-roast the coriander seeds until aromatic. Remove the coriander seeds and dry-roast the cumin, then the cinnamon. Grind the roasted spices and the cardamom to a fine powder using a spice grinder or mortar and pestle.

Blend all the marinade ingredients in a blender or food processor until smooth. If you don't have a blender, finely chop the onion, garlic and ginger and pound together in a mortar and pestle, or very finely chop all the large pieces with a knife and mix with the remaining marinade ingredients. Mix the paste thoroughly with the chicken strips. Cover and marinate in the fridge overnight.

Preheat a griddle or barbecue until it is very hot, or heat the grill (broiler) to its highest setting. Cook the chicken pieces for 4 minutes on each side on the griddle, or spread the pieces on a baking sheet and grill (broil) for about 8–10 minutes on each side, until almost black in patches.

spicy grilled chicken

vegetable bhaji

240 g (2¼ cups) besan flour
1 teaspoon chilli powder
1 teaspoon ground turmeric
¼ teaspoon asafoetida
100 g (1 cup) carrots, cut into thin sticks
100 g (1 cup) snowpeas (mangetout),
   cut into thin sticks
50 g (2 oz) thin eggplant (aubergine),
   cut into thin sticks
6 curry leaves
oil, for deep-frying

Makes 20

Mix together the besan flour, chilli powder, turmeric, asafoetida and a pinch of salt. Add enough water to make a thick batter that will hold the vegetables together. Mix the vegetables and curry leaves into the batter.

Fill a *karhai* or heavy-based saucepan to one-third full with oil and heat to 180°C (350°F/Gas 4), or until a cube of bread fries brown in 15 seconds when dropped in the oil. Lift clumps of vegetables out of the batter and lower carefully into the oil. Fry until golden all over and cooked through, then drain on paper towels. Sprinkle with salt and serve hot with chutney or raita.

500 g (1 lb 2 oz) potatoes, cut into pieces
150 g (1 cup) fresh or frozen peas
4 tablespoons oil
2 green chillies, finely chopped
½ red onion, finely chopped
2 cm (¾ in) piece of ginger, grated
1 teaspoon ground turmeric
1 teaspoon ground cumin
1 teaspoon ground coriander
½ teaspoon garam masala (page 251)
2 tablespoons besan flour
1 tablespoon lemon juice

Makes 24

Cook the potatoes in boiling water for 15 minutes, or until tender enough to mash. Drain well until they are dry but still hot. Cook the peas in boiling water for 4 minutes, or until tender, then drain.

Mash the potato in a large bowl and add the peas. Put 1 tablespoon of the oil in a small saucepan and fry the chilli, onion, ginger and spices for 1 minute, or until aromatic. Add them to the potato with the besan flour and mix. Mix in the lemon juice and some salt. Divide the potato into portions the size of golf balls and shape into patties.

Heat the remaining oil in a heavy-based frying pan (non-stick if you have one) and add the potato patties in batches. Fry them on each side until crisp and golden brown. Serve hot or cold in small dishes.

aloo ki tikki

pork tikka

MARINADE
1 onion, roughly chopped
3 garlic cloves, roughly chopped
5 cm (2 in) piece of ginger, roughly
  chopped
½ tablespoon ground cumin
1 teaspoon ground coriander
½ tablespoon garam masala (page 251)
¼ teaspoon chilli powder
pinch of ground black pepper
250 ml (1 cup) thick plain yoghurt
  or recipe page 250

500 g (1 lb 2 oz) pork tenderloin,
  centre cut, cut into 2.5 cm (1 in) cubes

SAUCE
1 large red onion, roughly chopped
1 garlic clove, roughly chopped
2.5 cm (1 in) piece of ginger, roughly
  chopped
1 green chilli, roughly chopped
25 g (¾ cup) coriander (cilantro) leaves

120 ml (½ cup) oil
1 tablespoon garam masala (page 251)

Serves 4

To prepare the marinade, finely chop the onion, garlic and ginger in a food processor or, if you don't have a processor, with a knife. Add the spices and yoghurt to the paste and mix through.

Put the pork in a bowl, add the marinade and mix well. Cover and marinate in the fridge for 2 hours or overnight.

To make the sauce, finely chop the onion, garlic, ginger, chilli and coriander in a food processor or, if you don't have a processor, with a knife.

Heat the oil in a heavy-based frying pan, large enough to fit the meat in a single layer, until sizzling but not smoking. Add the sauce and stir over medium heat for 2 minutes, or until softened but not brown. Increase the heat to high and add the pork with the marinade. Stir constantly for 5 minutes, then reduce the heat to medium and let the meat and its juices bubble away for 15–20 minutes, or until the liquid has completely evaporated. The meat and the dryish sauce will be a rich dark brown.

Season with salt, to taste, and sprinkle with the garam masala. Cook for another 2 minutes to allow the added seasoning to be absorbed.

PASTRY
450 g (1 lb) maida or plain
  (all-purpose) flour
1 teaspoon salt
4 tablespoons oil or ghee

FILLING
400 g (14 oz) potatoes, cut into quarters
80 g (½ cup) peas
1½ teaspoons cumin seeds
½ teaspoon coriander seeds
2 tablespoons oil

½ onion, finely chopped
¼ teaspoon ground turmeric
½ teaspoon garam masala (page 251)
2 green chillies, chopped
3 cm (1 in) piece of ginger, chopped
1½ tablespoons lemon juice
2 tablespoons chopped coriander
  (cilantro) leaves

oil, for deep-frying

Makes 30

To make the pastry, sift the maida and salt into a bowl, then rub in the oil until the mixture resembles breadcrumbs. Add 180–200 ml (¾–1 cup) warm water, a little at a time, to make a pliable dough. Turn out onto a floured surface and knead for 5 minutes, or until smooth. Cover and set aside for 15 minutes.

To make the filling, cook the potato in simmering water for 10 minutes, or until tender. Drain and cut into small cubes. Cook the peas in simmering water for 2 minutes. Drain and refresh in cold water.

Place a small frying pan over low heat, dry-roast the cumin seeds until aromatic, then remove. Dry-roast the coriander seeds. Grind ½ teaspoon of the cumin and all the coriander to a powder in a spice grinder or a mortar and pestle.

Heat the oil in a heavy-based saucepan over low heat and fry the onion until light brown. Stir in all the cumin, the coriander, turmeric and garam masala. Add the potato, chilli and ginger and stir for 1 minute. Mix in the lemon juice and coriander leaves and salt, to taste, then leave to cool.

On a floured surface, roll out one-third of the pastry to a 28 cm (11 in) circle, about 3 mm (⅛ in) thick. Cut 10 circles with an 8 cm (3 in) cutter and spoon ½ tablespoon of filling onto the centre of each. Moisten the edges with water, then fold over and seal with a fork into a semicircle. Repeat to use all the filling and pastry. Fill a *karhai* or heavy-based saucepan to one-third full with oil and heat to 180°C (350°F/Gas 4), or until a cube of bread fries brown in 15 seconds. Fry a few samosas at a time until browned. Turn and fry the other side. Drain on a wire rack for 5 minutes before draining on paper towels.

samosas

stuffed parathas

400 g (2²/₃ cups) atta (chapati) flour or
    200 g (1¹/₃ cups) wholemeal flour and
    200 g (1²/₃ cups) plain (all-purpose) flour
1 teaspoon salt
4 tablespoons oil or ghee
200 g (7 oz) potatoes, unpeeled
¹/₄ teaspoon mustard seeds
¹/₂ onion, finely chopped

pinch of ground turmeric
pinch of asafoetida
ghee or oil, for shallow-frying
extra ghee or oil, for brushing
    on the dough

Makes 14

Sift the atta and salt into a bowl and make a well in the centre. Add
2 tablespoons of the oil and about 290 ml (1¹/₄ cups) tepid water and mix to
a soft, pliable dough. Turn out onto a floured surface, knead for 5 minutes,
then place in an oiled bowl. Cover and allow to rest for 30 minutes.

Simmer the potatoes for 15–20 minutes or until cooked. Cool slightly, then
peel and mash. Heat the remaining oil in a saucepan over medium heat,
add the mustard seeds, cover and shake the pan until the seeds start to pop.
Add the onion and fry for 1 minute. Stir in the turmeric and asafoetida. Mix
in the potato and cook over low heat for 1–2 minutes, or until the mixture
leaves the side of the pan. Season with salt, to taste, and leave to cool.

Divide the dough into 14 portions and roll each into a 15 cm (6 in) circle.
Spread 1 teaspoon of the potato filling evenly over one half of each circle of
dough and fold into a semicircle. Rub oil on half the surface area, then fold
over into quarters. Roll out until doubled in size. Cover the parathas with a
cloth, then cook them one at a time.

Heat a *tava*, griddle or a heavy-based frying pan over medium heat. Brush
the surface of the *tava* or griddle with oil. Remove the excess flour on each
paratha prior to cooking by holding it in the palms of your hands and gently
slapping it from one hand to the other. If you leave the flour on it may burn.

Cook each paratha for 2–3 minutes, then turn over and cook for 1 minute, or
until the surface has brown flecks. Cooking should be quick to ensure the
parathas remain soft. Cover the cooked parathas with a cloth. Parathas must
be served warm. They can be reheated in a microwave, or wrapped in foil
and heated in a conventional oven at 180°C (350°F/Gas 4) for 10 minutes.

30 g (1½ cups) mint leaves
30 g (⅔ cup) coriander (cilantro) leaves
1 green chilli
1 tablespoon tamarind purée (page 250)
½ teaspoon salt
1½ teaspoons sugar
3 tablespoons thick plain yoghurt
 or recipe page 250 (optional)

Serves 4

Wash the mint and coriander leaves. Discard any tough stalks but keep the young soft ones for flavour. Blend all the ingredients together in a blender or food processor, or chop everything finely and pound it together in a mortar and pestle. Taste the chutney and add more salt if necessary. If you want a creamier, milder chutney, stir in the yoghurt.

mint and coriander chutney

a little taste of...

The Moghul Emperors arrived in North India from Central Asia in the 16th century, bringing fabulous wealth and a luxurious taste in palaces and gardens, culture and food. Court chefs were trained in the richly beautiful cooking style of Persia and soon incorporated native ingredients, especially India's herbs and spices, into their cooking. Created in the Emperors' kitchens, Moghul cuisine must be the world's most opulent: saffron, gold and silver leaf interlace savoury dishes and sweets; sauces and *kormas*, braised dishes, are made from cream, yoghurt and butter; and rice *pulaos* and *biryanis* are enriched with almonds, pistachios and dried fruit. The Moghuls were Muslims who loved eating meat, and most of India's meat dishes were originally the creation of an imperial chef. Moghul cuisine is also characterized by its fragrance, from the warm, spicy smells of cloves, cardamom, cinnamon and nutmeg to the floral aroma of rosewater. Today, Moghul cooking is India's 'classical cooking', enjoyed in the North, in the southern imperial city of Hyderabad, and in most Indian restaurants.

...the Moghul court

lamb kofta

1 small onion, roughly chopped
5 cm (2 in) piece of ginger,
    roughly chopped
2 garlic cloves, roughly chopped
2 green chillies, seeded and
    roughly chopped
15 g (½ cup) coriander (cilantro) leaves
2 tablespoons thick plain yoghurt
    or recipe page 250
500 g (1 lb 2 oz) minced lamb

2½ teaspoons ground cumin
1½ teaspoons ground coriander
2 teaspoons garam masala (page 251)
¼ teaspoon chilli powder
2½ teaspoons salt
½ teaspoon ground black pepper
3–4 tablespoons oil

Serves 6

Blend the onion, ginger, garlic, chopped chilli and the coriander leaves together in a food processor until they form a paste. If you don't have a food processor, use a mortar and pestle, or finely chop everything together with a knife. Add the yoghurt to the paste and mix well.

Put the lamb in a bowl, add the paste and mix by hand, kneading the ingredients into the meat until thoroughly combined. Add all the spices, and the salt and pepper, and mix again to distribute evenly. Cover and refrigerate for 1–2 hours to allow the flavours to develop and also to make the mixture firmer and therefore easier to handle.

Wet your hands and roll small handfuls (about a heaped tablespoon) of the mince mixture into small balls (wetting your hands prevents the mixture from sticking to your hands). You should have about 30–40 meatballs.

Heat 1 tablespoon of the oil in a large, heavy-based frying pan. When hot, but not smoking, add 10 meatballs in a single layer. Brown on all sides by gently shaking the pan for 2–3 minutes. Don't be tempted to turn them over with a spoon or they may break up. Test a kofta by breaking it open. If it is cooked through, there should be no pink meat inside. If the meat is still pink, cook for another minute or two. Remove and drain on paper towels. Repeat with the remaining meatballs. Serve with cocktail sticks for picking them up. Mint and coriander chutney (page 48) is the perfect accompaniment but other chutneys are also suitable.

2 cm (¾ in) piece of ginger,
  roughly chopped
3 garlic cloves, roughly chopped
75 g (½ cup) blanched almonds
150 ml (⅔ cup) thick plain yoghurt
  or recipe page 250
½ teaspoon chilli powder
¼ teaspoon ground cloves
¼ teaspoon ground cinnamon
1 teaspoon garam masala (page 251)
4 cardamom pods, lightly crushed

400 g (14 oz) tin chopped tomatoes
1¼ teaspoons salt
1 kg (2 lb 4 oz) chicken skinless, boneless
  thigh fillets, cut into fairly large pieces
5 tablespoons ghee or clarified butter
1 large onion, thinly sliced
6 tablespoons finely chopped coriander
  (cilantro) leaves
4 tablespoons thick (double/heavy) cream

Serves 6

Blend the ginger and garlic together to a paste in a food processor or use a mortar and pestle, or crush the garlic and finely grate the ginger and mix them together. Grind the almonds in a food processor or finely chop with a knife. Put the paste and almonds in a bowl with the yoghurt, chilli powder, cloves, cinnamon, garam masala, cardamom pods, tomato and salt, and blend together with a fork. Add the chicken pieces and stir to coat thoroughly. Cover and marinate for 2 hours, or overnight, in the fridge.

Preheat the oven to 180°C (350°F/Gas 4). Heat the ghee in a *karhai* or deep, heavy-based frying pan, add the onion and fry until softened and brown. Add the chicken mixture and fry for 2 minutes. Mix in the fresh coriander. Put the mixture into a shallow baking dish, pour in the cream and stir with a fork.

Bake for 1 hour. If the top is browning too quickly during cooking, cover with a piece of foil. Leave to rest for 10 minutes before serving. The oil will rise to the surface. Just before serving, place the dish under a hot grill (broiler) for about 2 minutes to brown the top. Before serving, slightly tip the dish and spoon off any excess oil.

butter chicken

chicken with coriander and almonds

1.5 kg (3 lb 5 oz) chicken or chicken pieces
50 g (⅓ cup) blanched almonds
2 onions, roughly chopped
4 garlic cloves, roughly chopped
2 green chillies, roughly chopped
5 cm (2 in) piece of ginger,
   roughly chopped
7 tablespoons oil or ghee
2 Indian bay leaves (cassia leaves)
1½ tablespoons ground coriander
1 tablespoon ground cumin

¼ teaspoon chilli powder
¼ teaspoon ground turmeric
¼ teaspoon paprika
2 teaspoons salt
1 teaspoon ground black pepper
4 tablespoons finely chopped coriander
   (cilantro) leaves
170 ml (⅔ cup) cream or thick
   (double/heavy) cream for thicker sauce

Serves 4

If using a whole chicken, cut it into eight pieces by removing both legs and cutting between the joint of the drumstick and thigh. Cut down either side of the backbone and remove the backbone. Turn the chicken over and cut through the cartilage down the centre of the breastbone. Cut each breast in half, leaving the wing attached to the top half. Trim off the wing tips.

Grind the almonds in a food processor or finely chop with a knife. Blend the onion, garlic, chilli and ginger together in a food processor until finely chopped, but not puréed, or finely chop them together with a knife.

Heat the oil in a *karhai* or heavy-based saucepan over medium heat, add the onion mixture and bay leaves and stir until lightly browned. Add the chicken to the pan and fry, turning constantly, for 10 minutes or until golden.

Add the coriander, cumin, chilli powder, turmeric, paprika, salt and pepper to the pan and stir with the chicken for 3 minutes until absorbed into the meat. Add 100 ml (½ cup) water, stirring the chicken for 5 minutes over medium heat. The water will have reduced to a rich, thick sauce. Add 150 ml (⅔ cup) water and bring to the boil. Reduce the heat, cover and simmer for 20 minutes. Add three-quarters of the coriander to the chicken and stir.

Blend the almonds with 140 ml (three-quarters) of the cream in a blender to form a smooth paste. If you don't have a blender, just mix the cream with the ground nuts. Add to the chicken, stir well and cook until heated through. Stir in the remaining cream before serving, to create a creamy, even sauce. Sprinkle with the remaining coriander.

8 garlic cloves, crushed
6 cm (2¼ in) piece of ginger, grated
2 teaspoons ground cumin
1 teaspoon Kashmiri chilli powder
2 teaspoons paprika
2 teaspoons ground coriander
1 kg (2 lb 4 oz) boneless leg or shoulder
    of lamb, cut into 3 cm (1 in) cubes
5 tablespoons ghee or oil
1 onion, finely chopped
6 cardamom pods

4 cloves
2 Indian bay leaves (cassia leaves)
8 cm (3 in) piece of cinnamon stick
200 ml (¾ cup) thick plain yoghurt
    or recipe page 250
4 strands saffron, mixed with
    2 tablespoons milk
¼ teaspoon garam masala (page 251)

Serves 6

Mix the garlic, ginger, cumin, chilli powder, paprika and coriander in a large bowl. Add the meat and stir thoroughly to coat the meat cubes. Cover and marinate for at least 2 hours, or overnight, in the fridge.

Heat the ghee in a *karhai* or heavy-based saucepan over low heat. Add the onion and cook for about 10 minutes, or until the onion is lightly browned. Remove from the pan.

Add the cardamom pods, cloves, bay leaves and cinnamon to the pan and fry for 1 minute. Increase the heat to high, add the meat and onion, then mix well and fry for 2 minutes. Stir well, then reduce the heat to low, cover and cook for 15 minutes. Uncover and fry for another 3 minutes, or until the meat is quite dry. Add 100 ml (½ cup) water, cover and cook for 5–7 minutes, until the water has evaporated and the oil separates out and floats on the surface. Fry the meat for another 1–2 minutes, then add 250 ml (1 cup) water. Cover and cook for 40–50 minutes, gently simmering until the meat is tender. The liquid will reduce considerably.

Stir in the yoghurt when the meat is almost tender, taking care not to allow the meat to catch on the base of the pan. Add the saffron and milk. Stir the mixture a few times to mix in the saffron. Season with salt, to taste. Remove from the heat and sprinkle with the garam masala.

rogan josh

curry

To many outside India, curry is Indian food. The word comes from the Tamil *kari*, meaning a spicy, soupy sauce ladled over rice. The Europeans, perhaps unable to discern the subtleties of Indian cooking, took the term to mean just about any spicy dish. In the colonial kitchens of India, a new kind of Anglo-Indian cooking was born and Indian chefs, adapting traditional recipes to their British employers' tastes, invented dishes ranging from kedgeree and mulligatawny soup to hot, turmeric-yellow 'curry and rice'.

On returning to Britain, members of the Raj set about creating a 'curry powder' to reproduce the taste of the spicy southern *kari* of their Indian territories. Authentic *kari podi* typically included curry leaves, coriander, cumin, turmeric, mustard seeds, pepper and fenugreek, and these spices except for, perhaps surprisingly, the curry leaves, became the basis of British curry powder as well. However, the two spice mixes could not have been more different. The traditional Indian *kari* was always freshly ground as needed, while the commercial curry powders were premixed and so lost much of their pungency. And while the Indians would never have dreamed of using the same masala for different dishes, the British added this powder to all types of meat or poultry dishes. The result was a kind of hot 'stew', traditionally served with some intriguing accompaniments such as desiccated coconut, raisins, hard-boiled egg and slices of banana.

lamb korma

1 kg (2 lb 4 oz) boneless leg or shoulder
   of lamb, cut into 2.5 cm (1 in) cubes
2 tablespoons thick plain yoghurt
   or recipe page 250
1 tablespoon coriander seeds
2 teaspoons cumin seeds
5 cardamom pods
2 onions
2 tablespoons grated coconut
1 tablespoon white poppy seeds
   (khus khus)

3 green chillies, roughly chopped
4 garlic cloves, crushed
5 cm (2 in) piece of ginger, grated
25 g (1 oz) cashew nuts
6 cloves
¼ teaspoon ground cinnamon
2 tablespoons oil

Serves 4

Put the meat in a bowl, add the yoghurt and mix to coat thoroughly.

Place a small frying pan over low heat and dry-roast the coriander seeds until aromatic. Remove and dry-roast the cumin seeds. Grind the roasted mixture to a fine powder using a spice grinder or mortar and pestle. Remove the seeds from the cardamom pods and grind them.

Roughly chop one onion and finely slice the other. Put the roughly chopped onion with the ground spices, coconut, poppy seeds, chilli, garlic, ginger, cashew nuts, cloves and cinnamon in a blender, add 150 ml (²⁄₃ cup) water and process to a smooth paste. If you don't have a blender, crush together in a mortar and pestle, or finely chop with a knife, before adding the water.

Heat the oil in a *karhai* or heavy-based saucepan over medium heat. Add the finely sliced onion and fry until lightly browned. Pour the blended mixture into the pan, season with salt and cook over low heat for 1 minute, or until the liquid evaporates and the sauce thickens. Add the lamb with the yoghurt and slowly bring to the boil. Cover tightly and simmer for 1½ hours, or until the meat is tender. Stir the meat occasionally to prevent it from sticking to the pan. If the water has evaporated during the cooking time, add 125 ml (½ cup) of water to make a sauce. The sauce should be quite thick.

SAUCE
2 large ripe tomatoes
1 tablespoon oil
1 onion, finely sliced
2 garlic cloves, chopped
2 cm (¾ in) piece of ginger, grated
1 teaspoon ground turmeric
1 teaspoon salt
½ teaspoon chilli powder (optional)
½ teaspoon sugar
1 teaspoon garam masala (page 251)
125 ml (½ cup) thick plain yoghurt
   or recipe page 250

KOFTAS
10 small eggs
1 onion, finely chopped
4 garlic cloves, crushed
1 teaspoon salt
½ teaspoon ground turmeric
1 teaspoon garam masala (page 251)
1 teaspoon chilli powder
550 g (1 lb 4 oz) minced lamb
3 tablespoons rice flour
oil, for deep-frying

Serves 4

To make the koftas, cook eight of the eggs in boiling water for 10 minutes to hard-boil, then cool them immediately in cold water to prevent grey rings from forming around the yolks. When cold, peel them. Mix the onion, garlic, salt, turmeric, garam masala and chilli powder in a bowl. Add the lamb and knead the mixture well. Beat one of the remaining eggs in a bowl and knead it into the mince. Divide the meat mixture into eight portions and shape each portion into a ball. Flatten a ball into a pancake on the palm of your hand and place a hard-boiled egg in the centre. Wrap the mixture around the egg, smoothing the outside of the kofta and distributing the meat evenly to make a smooth shape. Make the rest in the same way, then dust with rice flour.

Fill a *karhai* or deep, heavy-based saucepan to one-third full with oil and heat to 180°C (350°F/Gas 4), or until a cube of bread fries brown in 15 seconds. Beat the remaining egg with a little water. Dip each kofta in the beaten egg, then deep-fry one at a time until golden. Drain on paper towels.

To make the sauce, score a cross in the top of each tomato, then plunge into boiling water for 20 seconds. Drain, peel away from the cross, then finely chop the tomatoes, discarding cores and seeds and reserving any juices. Heat the oil in a *karhai* and fry the onion, garlic and ginger for 5 minutes. Stir in the turmeric, salt, chilli, sugar and garam masala, then add the tomato. Simmer for a few minutes, then stir in the yoghurt and 125 ml (½ cup) hot water. Simmer for 3 minutes, season, then add the koftas and simmer for 5 minutes on each side, or until warmed through. Cut the koftas in half and serve with the sauce.

VICTORIA EGG STALL
Prop:- M. MUCKSHED ALI.
FRESH EGG MERCHENT &
GENERAL ORDER SUPPLIERS.
10-11-S.S. HOGG MARKET, CALCUTTA-87.

nargisi kofta

pulao

500 g (2½ cups) basmati rice
1 teaspoon cumin seeds
4 tablespoons ghee or oil
2 tablespoons chopped almonds
2 tablespoons raisins or sultanas
2 onions, finely sliced
2 cinnamon sticks
5 cardamom pods
1 teaspoon sugar

1 tablespoon ginger juice (page 248)
15 saffron threads, soaked in
    1 tablespoon warm milk
2 Indian bay leaves (cassia leaves)
250 ml (1 cup) coconut milk
2 tablespoons fresh or frozen peas
rosewater (optional)

Serves 6

Wash the rice in a sieve under cold, running water until the water from the rice runs clear. Drain the rice and put in a saucepan, cover with water and soak for 30 minutes. Drain.

Place a frying pan over low heat and dry-roast the cumin seeds until aromatic.

Heat the ghee in a *karhai* or heavy-based frying pan and fry the almonds and raisins until browned. Remove from the pan, fry the onion in the same ghee until dark golden brown, then remove from the pan.

Add the rice, roasted cumin seeds, cinnamon, cardamom pods, sugar, ginger juice, saffron and salt to the pan and fry for 2 minutes, or until aromatic.

Add the bay leaves and coconut milk to the pan, then add enough water to come about 5 cm (2 in) above the rice. Bring to the boil, cover and cook over medium heat for 8 minutes, or until most of the water has evaporated.

Add the peas to the pan and stir well. Reduce the heat to very low and cook until the rice is cooked through. Stir in the fried almonds, raisins and onion, reserving some for garnishing. Drizzle with a few drops of rosewater if you would like a more perfumed dish.

மஹேஷ் எண்டர்பிரைஸ்

MAHESH *Enterprises*

FANCY PIECE GOODS MERCHANTS

100, GODOWN St. [I FLOOR]

1 kg (2 lb 4 oz) boneless lamb leg or
   shoulder, cut into 3 cm (1 in) cubes
8 cm (3 in) piece of ginger, grated
2 garlic cloves, crushed
2 tablespoons garam masala (page 251)
½ teaspoon chilli powder
½ teaspoon ground turmeric
4 green chillies, finely chopped
20 g (⅔ cup) chopped coriander
   (cilantro) leaves
15 g (¼ cup) chopped mint leaves
500 g (2½ cups) basmati rice
4 onions, thinly sliced

¼ teaspoon salt
120 ml (½ cup) oil
125 g (4½ oz) unsalted butter, melted
250 ml (1 cup) thick plain yoghurt
   or recipe page 250
½ teaspoon saffron strands, soaked in
   2 tablespoons hot milk

SEALING DOUGH
200 g (1⅓ cups) wholewheat flour
1 teaspoon salt

Serves 6

Mix the lamb in a bowl with the ginger, garlic, garam masala, chilli powder, turmeric, chilli, coriander and mint. Cover and marinate in the fridge overnight.

Wash the rice in a sieve under cold, running water until the water from the rice runs clear. Put the sliced onion in a sieve, sprinkle with the salt and leave for 10 minutes to drain off any liquid that oozes out. Rinse and pat dry.

Heat the oil and butter in a heavy-based saucepan, add the onion and fry for 10 minutes, or until golden. Drain through a sieve, reserving the oil and butter. Remove the lamb from the marinade, reserving the marinade, and fry in batches in a little of the oil and butter until browned. Transfer to a *degchi* (thick-based pot) or heavy casserole dish and add the onion, remaining marinade and the yoghurt, and cook over low heat for 30–40 minutes, or until the lamb is tender.

In a separate saucepan, boil enough water to cover the rice. Add the rice to the pan. Return the water to the boil, cook the rice for 5 minutes, then drain well and spread the rice evenly over the meat. Pour 2 tablespoons of the leftover oil and butter over the rice and drizzle with the saffron and milk.

To make the sealing dough, preheat the oven to 220°C (425°F/Gas 7). Make a dough by mixing the flour and salt with a little water. Roll the dough into a sausage shape and use to seal the lid onto the rim of the pot or casserole, pressing it along the rim where the lid meets the pot. Put the pot over high heat for 5 minutes to bring the contents to the boil, then transfer it to the oven for 40 minutes. Remove the pot and break the seal of dough.

lamb biryani

yakhni pulao

225 g (1 cup) basmati rice
500 ml (2 cups) chicken stock
6 tablespoons ghee or oil
5 cardamom pods
5 cm (2 in) piece of cinnamon stick
6 cloves
8 black peppercorns
4 Indian bay leaves (cassia leaves)
1 onion, finely sliced

Serves 4

Wash the rice in a sieve under cold running water until the water from the rice runs clear. Drain.

Heat the stock to near boiling point in a saucepan.

Meanwhile, heat 2 tablespoons of the ghee over medium heat in a large, heavy-based saucepan. Add the cardamom pods, cinnamon, cloves, peppercorns and bay leaves and fry for 1 minute. Reduce the heat to low, add the rice and stir constantly for 1 minute. Add the heated stock and some salt to the rice and bring rapidly to the boil. Cover and simmer over low heat for 15 minutes. Leave the rice to stand for 10 minutes before uncovering. Lightly fluff up the rice before serving.

Meanwhile, heat the remaining ghee in a frying pan over low heat and fry the onion until soft. Increase the heat and fry until the onion is dark brown. Drain on paper towels, then use as garnish.

1 teaspoon cumin seeds
10 g (½ cup) mint leaves, roughly chopped
15 g (½ cup) coriander (cilantro) leaves,
 roughly chopped
2 cm (¾ in) piece of ginger,
 roughly chopped
2 green chillies, roughly chopped
300 ml (1¼ cups) thick plain yoghurt
 or recipe page 250
300 ml (1¼ cups) buttermilk
1 onion, thinly sliced

Serves 4

Place a small frying pan over low heat and dry-roast the cumin seeds until aromatic. Grind the seeds to a fine powder in a spice grinder or use a mortar and pestle.

Chop the mint, coriander, ginger and chilli to a fine paste in a blender, or chop together finely with a knife. Add the yoghurt and buttermilk and a pinch of salt to the mixture and blend until all the ingredients are well mixed. Check the seasoning, adjust if necessary, then mix in the sliced onion and the ground cumin, reserving a little cumin to sprinkle on top.

churri

a little taste of...

Named after the metal platter it is served on, a *thali* is India's set lunch, an entire meal served at once with five or six delicious curries, chutneys, even a sweet, set around a mound of rice or some soft, buttery *roti*, bread. Any dish can be served as part of a thali, it's up to the chef, but perhaps the best come from Gujarat, the meal's birthplace, where the thali is associated with some of India's finest vegetarian food. A typical thali combines one or two dry vegetable dishes with a couple of saucy curries, some dal, a poppadom, spicy red pickle, cooling curds, and occasionally a sweet, all laid out on a platter or banana leaf, or spooned into *katoris*, tiny metal bowls. Eating a thali is an art in itself and diners are careful not to mix flavours. Instead, they pour a little of just one or two of the curries onto the rice, then scoop the rice up to eat from the fingertips. Curds or pickles are added to adjust the heat to personal preference. The Indian equivalent of the 'all-you-can-eat buffet', waiters hover to refill a favourite dish as soon as a mouthful has been eaten.

...thali

aloo gobi

3 tablespoons oil
½ teaspoon black mustard seeds
½ onion, finely chopped
200 g (7 oz) potatoes, cut into cubes
¼ teaspoon ground turmeric
1 teaspoon ground cumin
1 teaspoon ground coriander
1½ teaspoons garam masala (page 251)
4 ripe tomatoes, chopped
1 large cauliflower, about 1.25 kg
** (2 lb 12 oz), cut into florets**
2 cm (¾ in) piece of ginger
1 teaspoon sugar

Serves 4

Heat the oil in a *karhai* or deep, heavy-based frying pan over low heat. Add the mustard seeds, cover the pan and wait for the seeds to pop. Add the onion and potato and fry until lightly browned.

Add the turmeric, cumin, coriander and garam masala to the pan and fry for a couple of seconds. Add the tomato and stir until the spices are well mixed. Add the cauliflower florets and stir until well mixed. Stir in the ginger, sugar and 125 ml (½ cup) water, increase the heat to medium and bring to the boil. Reduce the heat, cover and simmer for 15 minutes, or until the vegetables are tender. Season with salt, to taste.

Uncover the pan and if the sauce is too runny, simmer it for 1–2 minutes before serving.

600 g (1 lb 5 oz) (2 large) eggplants
   (aubergines)
1 red onion, chopped
1 garlic clove, chopped
2.5 cm (1 in) piece of ginger, chopped
1 green chilli, chopped
100 ml (½ cup) oil
¼ teaspoon chilli powder
½ teaspoon garam masala (page 251)
2 teaspoons ground cumin
2 teaspoons ground coriander
2 teaspoons salt
½ teaspoon ground black pepper
2 ripe tomatoes, chopped
3–4 tablespoons coriander (cilantro)
   leaves, finely chopped

Serves 4

Scorch the eggplants by holding them over a medium gas flame, or heating them under a grill (broiler) or on an electric hotplate. Keep turning them until the skin is blackened on all sides. Set aside until cool, then peel off the charred skin. Roughly chop the flesh. Don't worry if black specks remain on the flesh because they add to the smoky flavour.

Combine the onion, garlic, ginger and chilli in a blender and process until chopped together but not forming a paste. Alternatively, chop finely with a knife and mix in a bowl.

Heat the oil in a deep, heavy-based frying pan over medium heat, add the onion mixture and cook until slightly browned. Add all the spices, and the salt and pepper, and stir for 1 minute. Add the chopped tomato and simmer until the liquid has reduced. Put the eggplants in the pan and mash them with a wooden spoon, stirring around with the spices. Simmer for 10 minutes, or until the eggplants are soft.

Stir in the chopped coriander leaves and season with salt, to taste.

smoky spiced eggplant

saag paneer

500 g (1 bunch) English spinach leaves
½ teaspoon ground cumin
½ teaspoon ground coriander
½ teaspoon fenugreek seeds
1 tablespoon oil
1 red onion, thinly sliced
5 garlic cloves, chopped
200 g (7 oz) tin chopped tomatoes
2 cm (¾ in) piece of ginger, grated
1 teaspoon garam masala (page 251)
225 g (8 oz) paneer or ½ quantity of
   recipe (page 249), cubed

Serves 4

Blanch the spinach leaves in boiling water for 2 minutes, then refresh in cold water, drain and very finely chop. Place a small frying pan over low heat and dry-roast the cumin until aromatic. Remove, dry-roast the coriander, then the fenugreek.

Heat the oil in a *karhai* or heavy-based frying pan over low heat and fry the onion, garlic, cumin, coriander and fenugreek until brown and aromatic. Stir in the tomato, ginger and garam masala and bring to the boil. Add the spinach and cook until the liquid has reduced. Fold in the paneer, trying to keep it in whole pieces. Stir gently until heated through. Season with salt, to taste.

8 eggs
oil, for deep-frying
2 ripe tomatoes
25 g (1 oz) ghee
1 onion, finely chopped
1 garlic clove, finely chopped
400 ml (1¾ cups) coconut milk
1 teaspoon ground turmeric
½ teaspoon cayenne pepper
6 curry leaves

Serves 4

Put the eggs in a saucepan of water and bring to the boil. Boil for 6 minutes, until medium-hard, then cool quickly in a bowl of cold water. Shell them. You can now deep-fry the eggs if you wish. Fill a *karhai* or heavy-based saucepan to one-third full with oil and heat to 170°C (325°F/Gas 3), or until a cube of bread fries brown in 20 seconds when dropped in the oil. Fry the eggs in batches until they are golden and crisp. Drain on paper towels. Cut each egg in half if you prefer.

Score a cross in the top of each tomato. Plunge into boiling water for about 20 seconds, then drain and peel away from the cross. Roughly chop the tomatoes, discarding the cores and seeds.

Melt the ghee in a *karhai* or heavy-based frying pan over low heat, add the onion and garlic and cook until soft and golden. Add the tomato and cook until soft. Gradually stir in the coconut milk, then the turmeric and cayenne and season with salt. Bring to the boil and simmer for 2–3 minutes, until the sauce thickens slightly. Add the eggs and heat gently for 2–3 minutes. Garnish with the curry leaves.

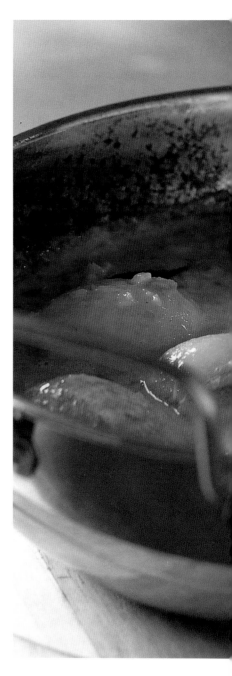

golden egg curry

basmati... The most refined of all rices, basmati is slender and perfumed, a prince among India's many varieties, which range from the dusty unpolished red rice of rural India to the cheap yet tasty Patna rice. True basmati is grown only in northern India, most famously around the city of Dehra Dun, and it is cultivated in terraces that tumble down the Himalayan foothills, the rice watered by pure snow-fed mountain rivers. Basmati's name comes from the Hindi for fragrance, and this wonderfully aromatic rice has a reputation for being delicate and difficult to grow, usually producing just one crop each year. Like wine, the climate, soil and farming methods can all affect its quality.

Despite growing one of the world's great varieties, India's North does not revere rice, unlike other parts of Asia. Instead, breads are the life-sustaining staple, and expensive basmati tends to be treated more as an ingredient, made into highly spiced *pulaos* and *biryanis*.

These rice dishes are a reminder of the North's Moghul past, and in today's India are a speciality of the Muslim cities of Delhi, Lucknow and Hyderabad. Their essential character lies in the way the rice is cooked so that each grain remains separate, not sticky. To achieve this, pulao rice is always a high-quality long grain, the best being aged basmati rice, stored after harvesting to enhance its distinctive aroma and decrease its moisture content. Before cooking, the rice is washed and sometimes soaked to rid it of any surface starch, then fried to keep the grains separate. Flavoured with spices, dried fruit, nuts, and often an extravagant amount of meat, these rice dishes share more culinary heritage with the Middle East than indigenous Indian rice cookery.

In the South, East and West of India, rice is the fundamental staple served at practically every meal, its importance to the diet underlined by its plain presentation. Curries are served with long-grain rice, which is capable of absorbing enough liquid to be scooped up by hand. There is no particular attempt made to keep the rice grains separate and, indeed, in the South rice is often ground down to make uniquely Indian rice batters for delicious *idlis* and *dosas*.

cauliflower
with mustard

2 teaspoons yellow mustard seeds
2 teaspoons black mustard seeds
1 teaspoon ground turmeric
1 teaspoon tamarind purée (page 250)
2–3 tablespoons mustard oil or oil
2 garlic cloves, finely chopped
½ onion, finely chopped
600 g (1 lb 5 oz) cauliflower, broken into
   small florets
3 mild green chillies, seeded and finely
   chopped
2 teaspoons kalonji (nigella seeds)

Serves 4

Grind the mustard seeds together to a fine powder in a spice grinder
or use a mortar and pestle. Mix with the turmeric, tamarind purée and
100 ml (½ cup) water to form a smooth liquid paste.

Heat 2 tablespoons oil in a *karhai* or large, heavy-based saucepan over
medium heat until almost smoking. Reduce the heat to low, add the garlic
and onion and fry until golden. Cook the cauliflower in batches, adding
more oil if necessary, and fry until lightly browned. Add the chilli and fry
for 1 minute, or until tinged with brown around the edges.

Return all the cauliflower to the pan, sprinkle it with the mustard mixture and
kalonji and stir well. Increase the heat to medium and bring to the boil, even
though there's not much sauce. Reduce the heat to low, cover and cook until
the cauliflower is nearly tender and the seasoning is dry. You may have to
sprinkle more water on the cauliflower as it cooks to stop it sticking to the pan.
If there is still excess liquid when the cauliflower is cooked, simmer with the
lid off until it dries out. Season with salt, to taste, and remove from the heat.

200 g (7 oz) potatoes
200 g (3 bunches) dill
2 tablespoons oil
2 garlic cloves, chopped
¼ teaspoon ground turmeric
1 teaspoon black mustard seeds
pinch of asafoetida
1 dried chilli

Serves 2

Cut the potatoes into 2.5 cm (1 in) cubes and cook in a saucepan of simmering water for 15 minutes or until just tender. Drain well.

Wash the dill in several changes of water and trim off the tough stalks. Roughly chop the dill.

Heat the oil in a heavy-based saucepan, add the garlic and fry for 30 seconds over low heat. Add the turmeric, mustard seeds, asafoetida and the whole chilli, cover and briefly allow the seeds to pop. Stir in the potato until well mixed. Add the dill, cover and cook over low heat for 5 minutes. The dill contains sufficient moisture to cook without the addition of any water. Season with salt, to taste.

shebu bhaji

matar paneer

225 g (8 oz) paneer or ½ quantity
  of recipe (page 249)
2 tablespoons ghee
50 g (2 oz) onion, chopped
200 g (1⅓ cups) fresh or frozen peas
½ teaspoon sugar
5 cm (2 in) piece of ginger, grated
2–3 green chillies, finely chopped
1 spring onion (scallion), finely chopped
½ teaspoon garam masala (page 251)
1 tablespoon chopped coriander
  (cilantro) leaves

Serves 4

Cut the paneer into 2 cm (1 in) cubes. Heat the ghee in a *karhai* or heavy-based frying pan over medium heat and carefully fry the paneer until golden on all sides. Remove from the pan.

Fry the onion lightly in the same ghee, until softened and lightly golden. Remove the onion from the pan. Add 5 tablespoons hot water and a pinch of salt to the ghee and simmer for 1 minute. Add the peas and sugar, cover and cook for 5–6 minutes, until the peas are almost cooked.

Add the onion, paneer, ginger, chilli and spring onion to the pan and cook for 2–3 minutes. Add the garam masala and coriander leaves. Season with salt, to taste.

½ **onion, roughly chopped**
1 **garlic clove, roughly chopped**
2.5 cm (1 in) **piece of ginger, chopped**
2 **green chillies, seeded and chopped**
4 **tablespoons oil**
1 **teaspoon cumin seeds**
1 **teaspoon ground turmeric**
500 g (1 lb 2 oz) **green cabbage,**
    finely shredded
1 **teaspoon salt**
½ **teaspoon ground black pepper**
2 **teaspoons ground cumin**
1 **teaspoon ground coriander**
¼ **teaspoon chilli powder**
20 g (1 oz) **unsalted butter**

Serves 4

Put the onion, garlic, ginger and chilli in a food processor and chop until finely chopped but not a paste, or chop together with a knife.

Heat the oil in a *karhai* or heavy-based frying pan over low heat and fry the onion mixture until softened but not browned. Add the cumin seeds and turmeric to the pan and stir for 1 minute. Mix in the cabbage, stirring thoroughly until all the leaves are coated in the yellow paste. Add the salt, pepper, cumin, coriander and chilli powder. Stir to coat the cabbage well, then cook for 10 minutes with the pan partially covered, stirring occasionally until the cabbage is soft. If the cabbage becomes too dry and starts sticking to the pan, add 1–2 tablespoons water. Stir in the butter and season with salt, to taste.

punjabi cabbage

saag gosht

2 teaspoons coriander seeds
1½ teaspoons cumin seeds
3 tablespoons oil
1 kg (2 lb 4 oz) boneless leg or shoulder
   of lamb, cut into 2.5 cm (1 in) cubes
4 onions, finely chopped
6 cloves
6 cardamom pods
10 cm (4 in) piece of cinnamon stick
10 black peppercorns
4 Indian bay leaves (cassia leaves)

3 teaspoons garam masala (page 251)
¼ teaspoon ground turmeric
1 teaspoon paprika
8 cm (3 in) piece of ginger, grated
4 garlic cloves, crushed
190 ml (¾ cup) thick plain yoghurt
   or recipe page 250
450 g (1 bunch) English spinach or
   amaranth leaves, roughly chopped

Serves 6

Place a small frying pan over low heat and dry-roast the coriander seeds until aromatic. Remove them and dry-roast the cumin seeds. Grind the roasted seeds to a fine powder using a spice grinder or mortar and pestle.

Heat the oil in a *karhai* or heavy-based saucepan over low heat and fry a few pieces of meat at a time until browned. Remove from the pan. Add more oil to the pan, if necessary, and fry the onion, cloves, cardamom pods, cinnamon stick, peppercorns and bay leaves until the onion is lightly browned. Add the cumin and coriander, garam masala, turmeric and paprika and fry for 30 seconds. Add the meat, ginger, garlic, yoghurt and 425 ml (1⅔ cups) water and bring to the boil. Reduce the heat to a simmer, cover and cook for 1½–2 hours, or until the meat is very tender. At this stage, most of the water should have evaporated. If it hasn't, remove the lid, increase the heat and fry until the moisture has evaporated. Season with salt, to taste.

Cook the spinach briefly in a little simmering water until it is just wilted, then refresh in cold water. Drain thoroughly, then finely chop. Squeeze out any extra water by putting the spinach between two plates and pushing them together.

Add the spinach to the lamb and cook for 3 minutes, or until the spinach and lamb are well mixed and any extra liquid has evaporated.

**800 g (1 lb 12 oz) eggplants (aubergines),
cut into wedges 4–5 cm (1½–2 in) long**
**400 g (14 oz) ripe tomatoes or 400 g
(14 oz) tin chopped tomatoes**
2.5 cm (1 in) piece of ginger, grated
6 garlic cloves, crushed
300 ml (1¼ cups) oil
1 teaspoon fennel seeds

½ teaspoon kalonji (nigella seeds)
1 tablespoon ground coriander
¼ teaspoon ground turmeric
½ teaspoon cayenne pepper
1 teaspoon salt

Serves 6

Put the eggplant pieces in a colander, sprinkle them with salt and leave them for 30 minutes to allow any bitter juices to run out. Rinse, squeeze out any excess water, then pat dry with paper towels. If using fresh tomatoes, score a cross in the top of each and plunge into boiling water for 20 seconds. Drain and peel away from the cross. Roughly chop the tomatoes, discarding the cores and seeds and reserving any juices.

Purée the ginger and garlic with one-third of the tomato in a blender or food processor. If you don't have a blender, finely chop the tomatoes and mix with the ginger and garlic.

Heat 125 ml (½ cup) of the oil in a large, deep, heavy-based frying pan and when hot, add as many eggplant pieces as you can fit in a single layer. Cook over medium heat until brown on both sides, then transfer to a sieve over a bowl so the excess oil can drain off. Add the remaining oil to the pan as needed and cook the remaining eggplant in batches.

Reheat the oil that's left in the pan and add the fennel seeds and kalonji. Cover and allow to pop for a few seconds. Add the tomato and ginger mixture and the remaining ingredients, except the eggplant. Cook, stirring regularly for 5–6 minutes, until the mixture becomes thick and fairly smooth (be careful as it may spit at you). Carefully add the cooked eggplant so the pieces stay whole, then cover the pan and cook gently for about 10 minutes.

Store the eggplant in the sauce in the fridge. Pour off any excess oil before serving. The eggplant can either be served cold or gently warmed through.

spicy eggplant

bhindi masala

500 g (1 lb 2oz) okra, about
   5 cm (2 in) long
3 green chillies
3 tablespoons oil
1 teaspoon black mustard seeds
1 red onion, finely chopped
1 teaspoon ground cumin
1 teaspoon ground coriander
2 teaspoons garam masala (page 251)
1 teaspoon ground turmeric
4 garlic cloves, finely chopped

Serves 4

Wash the okra and pat dry with paper towels. Trim the tops and tails. Ignore any sticky, glutinous liquid that appears because this will disappear as the okra cooks.

Cut the chillies in half lengthwise, leaving them attached at the stalk, and scrape out any seeds. Heat the oil in a *karhai* or deep, heavy-based frying pan, add the mustard seeds and onion and cook until the seeds pop and the onion is light brown. Add the cumin, coriander, garam masala and turmeric and cook until the popping stops.

Add the garlic, okra and the chilli to the pan, fry for 5 minutes, stir and cook for 2 minutes. Add 60 ml (¼ cup) water, 1 tablespoon at a time, and stir to make a sauce. Season with salt, to taste. Simmer for about 15 minutes, until the okra is cooked through and the sauce is thick and dry.

500 g (1 lb 2 oz) tiger prawns
1½ tablespoons lemon juice
3 tablespoons oil
½ onion, finely chopped
½ teaspoon ground turmeric
5 cm (2 in) piece of cinnamon stick
4 cloves
7 cardamom pods
5 Indian bay leaves (cassia leaves)
2 cm (¾ in) piece of ginger, grated
3 garlic cloves, chopped
1 teaspoon chilli powder
50 g (2 oz) creamed coconut
   mixed with 150 ml (⅔ cup) water,
   or 150 ml (⅔ cup) coconut milk

Serves 4

Peel and devein the prawns, leaving the tails intact. Put them in a bowl, add the lemon juice, then toss together and leave them for 5 minutes. Rinse the prawns under running cold water and pat dry with paper towels.

Heat the oil in a *karhai* or heavy-based frying pan and fry the onion until lightly browned. Add the turmeric, cinnamon, cloves, cardamom, bay leaves, ginger and garlic, and fry for 1 minute. Add the chilli powder, creamed coconut or coconut milk, and salt, to taste, and slowly bring to the boil. Reduce the heat and simmer for 2 minutes. Add the prawns, return to the boil, then reduce the heat and simmer for 5 minutes, or until the prawns are cooked through and the sauce is thick.

creamy prawn curry

cardamom chicken

1.5 kg (3 lb 5 oz) chicken or chicken pieces
25 cardamom pods
4 garlic cloves, crushed
3 cm (1 in) piece of ginger, grated
300 ml (1¼ cups) thick plain yoghurt
 or recipe page 250
1½ teaspoons ground black pepper
grated rind of 1 lemon
2 tablespoons ghee or oil
400 ml (1⅔ cups) coconut milk
6 green chillies, pricked all over
2 tablespoons chopped coriander
 (cilantro) leaves
3 tablespoons lemon juice

Serves 4

If using a whole chicken, cut it into eight pieces by removing both legs and cutting between the joint of the drumstick and thigh. Cut down either side of the backbone and remove the backbone. Turn the chicken over and cut through the cartilage down the centre of the breastbone. Cut each breast in half, leaving the wing attached to the top half. Trim off the wing tips. Remove the skin if you prefer.

Remove the seeds from the cardamom pods and crush them in a spice grinder or use a mortar and pestle. In a blender, mix the garlic and ginger with enough of the yoghurt (about 50 ml or ¼ cup) to make a paste, or, if you prefer, mix them with a spoon. Add the cardamom, pepper and grated lemon rind. Spread this over the chicken pieces, cover, and leave in the fridge overnight.

Heat the ghee in a *karhai* or heavy-based frying pan over low heat and brown the chicken pieces all over. Add the remaining yoghurt and coconut milk to the pan, bring to the boil, then add the whole chillies and the coriander leaves. Simmer for 20–30 minutes or until the chicken is cooked through. Season with salt, to taste, and stir in the lemon juice.

spice box... The Indian chef's spice box is a tool kit — the roots, leaves, buds, stems, bark and seeds are the building blocks of Indian cooking. The spices are fresh and kept whole to prevent them from turning stale and those that need to be ground are dry-roasted first to develop their flavour, then crushed before cooking. Heating spices makes them digestible and aromatic, and in Indian cooking the sequence of adding them is usually the same. Whole spices are cooked in hot oil, then any wet spices, such as onion, garlic and ginger, are chopped into a paste and added. Finally, the ground spices are stirred in. The Indian cook uses an amazing variety of spices, but a few are essential spices, used in most curries.

asafoetida This foul-smelling, yellow-coloured spice is the dried latex of a type of fennel. It is fried with whole spices to temper its odour, a tiny pinch enough to impart a garlicky onion taste, an important flavour in strict vegetarian cooking.

chilli powder This has become a basic Indian spice, and either the powder or fresh green chillies are used to make virtually all Indian dishes. Adding a pungent hot taste, this is one spice that can be added during cooking, adjusting the heat of a dish.

coriander seeds Both the seeds and leaves are India's most widely used flavouring; the seeds add a cooling flavour and sweet aroma to most savoury dishes. Coriander is also a key ingredient in spice mixes such as garam masala. Along with cumin and turmeric, it is the flavour that defines North Indian cooking.

cumin seeds Almost all Indian curries begin with either cumin or mustard seeds crackling in hot oil. And surprisingly, their strong, slightly bitter smell is one that many people dislike. Cumin seeds have a hot, pungent taste.

mustard seeds An essential taste in the cooking of southern and western India, mustard seeds add a nutty rather than mustard-hot flavour. In the South, they are tempered in hot oil until they pop and give out an earthy aroma, while in Bengal they are crushed into a hot paste and often combined with mustard oil.

turmeric Turmeric is perhaps India's most important spice, the essence of almost every curry. It has a mild taste and a lingering aroma, and just a little is needed to balance out and enhance the flavour of other spices, as well as giving a curry its characteristic golden colour. It is not added to green vegetables, as it turns them grey.

140 ml (²/₃ cup) oil
1 large onion, chopped
4 garlic cloves, crushed
8 cm (3 in) piece of ginger, chopped
2 Indian bay leaves (cassia leaves)
600 g (1 lb 5 oz) pork sparerib chops,
    bones removed, meat cut into
    2 cm (¾ in) cubes
pinch of asafoetida
1 teaspoon chilli powder
½ teaspoon ground turmeric
1½ tablespoons ground cumin
1½ tablespoons ground coriander
½ teaspoon garam masala (page 251)
1½ tablespoons lemon juice
4 dried chillies
1 teaspoon kalonji (nigella seeds)

1 teaspoon yellow mustard seeds
2 tomatoes, finely chopped
4 green chillies
2 teaspoons paprika
2 red capsicum (peppers), cut into
    2.5 cm (1 in) pieces
2 green capsicum (peppers), cut into
    2.5 cm (1 in) pieces
1 tablespoon salt
1 teaspoon ground black pepper
500 g (1 lb 2 oz) potatoes, cut into
    2.5 cm (1 in) cubes
10 curry leaves
1 teaspoon garam masala (page 251)

Serves 6

Heat 100 ml (½ cup) of the oil in a *karhai* or deep, heavy-based frying pan over medium heat. Add half of each of the onion, garlic and ginger, and the bay leaves and fry for 2 minutes, or until the onion is soft. Increase the heat to high, add the meat and asafoetida and fry for 2 minutes, stirring until the meat is brown. Reduce the heat to medium and cook for 10 minutes. Remove from the heat, lift out the meat with a spatula and place in a bowl. Add the chilli powder, turmeric, 1¼ tablespoons cumin, 2 teaspoons coriander and the garam masala to the meat, and stir. Stir in the lemon juice.

Heat the remaining oil in the same pan over medium heat and fry the remaining onion, garlic and ginger for a few minutes until the onion is soft. Add the dried chillies, kalonji, mustard seeds and the remaining coriander and cumin. Fry for 2 minutes, or until the seeds start to pop. Add the tomato and fry for 1 minute. Reduce the heat and cook for 5 minutes, or until the liquid has reduced. Stir in the green chillies and the paprika. Add the meat and stir over medium heat for 2 minutes, or until all the sauce has been absorbed. Add the capsicum, then reduce the heat to simmering and cover the pan. Cook for 10 minutes, then add the salt, pepper and cubed potato. Add 100 ml (½ cup) water, cover and simmer for 1 hour, stirring occasionally. Add the curry leaves and cook for 15 minutes. The meat and potato should be very tender, but if not, cook for another 15 minutes. Add the garam masala and season with salt, to taste.

pork with capsicum and potatoes

kheema matar

2 onions, roughly chopped
4 garlic cloves, roughly chopped
5 cm (2 in) piece of ginger,
   roughly chopped
4 green chillies
160 ml (²/₃ cup) oil
2 Indian bay leaves (cassia leaves)
500 g (1 lb 2 oz) minced lamb
pinch of asafoetida
2 tablespoons tomato purée
¹/₄ teaspoon ground turmeric
¹/₂ teaspoon chilli powder

2 tablespoons ground coriander
2 tablespoons ground cumin
2 tablespoons thick plain yoghurt
   or recipe page 250
3 teaspoons salt
1 teaspoon ground black pepper
225 g (1¹/₂ cups) fresh or frozen peas
¹/₄ teaspoon garam masala (page 251)
5 tablespoons finely chopped coriander
   (cilantro)

Serves 4

Put the onion, garlic, ginger and two of the chillies in a food processor and process until very finely chopped. If you don't have a food processor, finely chop the ingredients or grind them together in a mortar and pestle.

Heat the oil in a *karhai* or heavy-based frying pan over medium heat, add the onion mixture and bay leaves and fry for 3–4 minutes, or until golden brown. Add the lamb mince and fry for 15 minutes, stirring occasionally to prevent the meat from sticking. Break up any lumps of mince with the back of a fork. During this time, the flavours of the onion, garlic, ginger and chilli will infuse into the meat. Add the asafoetida and tomato purée, stir and lower the heat to a simmer.

Add the turmeric, chilli powder, coriander and cumin and stir for 1 minute. Add the yoghurt, salt and pepper and continue frying for 5 minutes. Add 200 ml (³/₄ cup) water, a little at a time, stirring after each addition until it is well absorbed. Add the peas and the two remaining whole chillies. Stir well, then cover and simmer for 20 minutes, or until the peas are cooked through. If using frozen peas, cook the mince and chillies for 20 minutes and add the peas 5 minutes before the end of cooking. Add the garam masala and chopped coriander and stir for 1 minute before serving.

1½ teaspoons cumin seeds
2½ teaspoons coriander seeds
4 garlic cloves, roughly chopped
8 cm (3 in) piece of ginger,
   roughly chopped
400 g (14 oz) onions, finely chopped
3 tablespoons oil
1 kg (2 lb 4 oz) boneless leg of lamb, cut
   into 3 cm (1 in) cubes
2 teaspoons garam masala (page 251)
1 teaspoon ground turmeric

Serves 4

Place a small frying pan over low heat and dry-roast the cumin seeds until aromatic. Remove, then dry-roast the coriander seeds. Grind the roasted mixture to a fine powder using a spice grinder or mortar and pestle. In a food processor or with a knife, finely chop together the garlic, ginger and two-thirds of the onion.

Heat the oil in a *karhai* or deep, heavy-based frying pan and fry the remaining onion until golden brown. Add the lamb and cook until the meat is brown all over. Stir in the cumin and coriander, garam masala and turmeric. Add the onion, ginger and garlic mixture and 250 ml (1 cup) water and bring slowly to the boil. Cover tightly, reduce the heat to a simmer and cook for 1 hour, or until the meat is very tender. If the liquid evaporates quickly, add 125 ml (½ cup) hot water. When the meat is cooked, it should have a thick coating sauce. If the sauce is too thin, simmer for a few minutes with the lid off. Season with salt, to taste.

do piaza

lamb
madras

1 kg (2 lb 4 oz) boneless leg or shoulder
   of lamb, cut into 2.5 cm (1 in) cubes
1½ teaspoons ground turmeric
2 tablespoons coriander seeds
2 teaspoons cumin seeds
10 dried chillies
12 curry leaves
10 garlic cloves, roughly chopped
5 cm (2 in) piece of ginger,
   roughly chopped
1 teaspoon fennel seeds

1 tablespoon tamarind purée (page 250)
4 tablespoons oil or ghee
3 large onions, sliced
600 ml (2½ cups) coconut milk
8 cm (3 in) piece of cinnamon stick
6 cardamom pods
curry leaves, to garnish

Serves 6

Rub the cubed lamb with the ground turmeric. Place a small frying pan over low heat and dry-roast the coriander seeds until aromatic. Remove and dry-roast the cumin seeds, then repeat with the chillies. Grind them all to a powder in a spice grinder or use a mortar and pestle. Add six curry leaves, the garlic and ginger and grind to a paste.

Dry-roast the fennel seeds in the pan until they brown and start to pop. Dissolve the tamarind in 125 ml (½ cup) hot water.

Heat the oil in a *karhai* or deep, heavy-based frying pan over low heat and fry the onion for 5–10 minutes or until soft. Add the chilli paste and cook for a few minutes or until aromatic. Add the meat and toss well to mix with the paste. Add 500 ml (2 cups) of the coconut milk and 60 ml (¼ cup) water. Bring to the boil and simmer over medium heat for 10 minutes, or until the liquid has reduced.

When the liquid has reduced, add the remaining coconut milk, the cinnamon stick, cardamom pods and fennel seeds. Season with salt and pepper. Partially cover the pan with a lid and cook over medium heat for 1 hour or until the meat is tender, stirring occasionally. When the meat is tender, add the tamarind purée and check the seasoning. Stir until the oil separates from the meat, then spoon it off or blot with paper towels before removing the pan from the heat.

Stir well and add the remaining six curry leaves. Garnish with curry leaves.

225 g (1 cup) masoor dal (red lentils)
1 onion, roughly chopped
1 ripe tomato, roughly chopped
50 g (2 oz) creamed coconut, mixed
   with 250 ml (1 cup) water, or
   250 ml (1 cup) coconut milk
2 green chillies, chopped
¼ teaspoon ground turmeric
½ teaspoon ground cumin
½ teaspoon ground coriander
2 tablespoons oil
1 teaspoon cumin seeds
½ teaspoon black mustard seeds
1 onion, very finely chopped
10 curry leaves

Serves 4

Put the lentils in a heavy-based saucepan with 500 ml (2 cups) water. Add the roughly chopped onion, tomato, creamed coconut or coconut milk, chillies, turmeric, cumin and coriander, and bring to the boil. Simmer and cook, stirring occasionally until the lentils are cooked to a soft mush (masoor dal does not hold its shape when it cooks). This will take about 25 minutes. If all the water has evaporated before the lentils are cooked, add an extra 125 ml (½ cup) of boiling water.

For the final seasoning (*tarka*), heat the oil in a small saucepan over low heat. Add the cumin seeds and mustard seeds, cover and allow the seeds to pop. Add the finely chopped onion and curry leaves and fry over low heat until the onion is golden brown. Pour the seasoned onions into the simmering lentils. Season with salt, to taste, and cook for another 5 minutes.

parippu

toor dal

500 g (2 cups) toor dal (yellow lentils)
5 x 5 cm (2 in) pieces of kokum
2 teaspoons coriander (cilantro) seeds
2 teaspoons cumin seeds
2 tablespoons oil
2 teaspoons black mustard seeds
10 curry leaves
7 cloves
10 cm (4 in) piece of cinnamon stick
5 green chillies, finely chopped
½ teaspoon ground turmeric
400 g (14 oz) tin chopped tomatoes
20 g (½ oz) jaggery or 10 g (¼ oz)
  molasses
coriander (cilantro) leaves

Serves 8

Soak the lentils in cold water for 2 hours. Rinse the kokum, remove any stones and put the kokum in a bowl with cold water for a few minutes to soften. Drain the lentils and put them in a heavy-based saucepan with 1 litre (4 cups) of water and the pieces of kokum. Bring slowly to the boil, then simmer for about 40 minutes, or until the lentils feel soft when pressed between the thumb and index finger.

Place a small frying pan over low heat and dry-roast the coriander seeds until aromatic. Remove and dry-roast the cumin seeds. Grind the roasted seeds to a fine powder using a spice grinder or mortar and pestle.

For the final seasoning (*tarka*), heat the oil in a small pan over low heat. Add the mustard seeds and allow to pop. Add the curry leaves, cloves, cinnamon, chillies, turmeric and the roasted spice mix and cook for 1 minute. Add the tomato and cook for 2–3 minutes until the tomato is soft and can be broken up easily and incorporated into the sauce. Add the jaggery, then pour the spicy mixture into the simmering lentils and cook for another 10 minutes. Season with salt, to taste. Garnish with coriander leaves.

dal

Dal is the dish that gastronomically unites India. A stew, made from peas, beans or lentils, it is eaten every day in almost every Indian household. *Dal roti*, dal with bread, is India's basic survival meal, one that provides many, especially India's vegetarians, with the main source of protein in their diet.

Dal is the name given to both the ingredient and the dish. The ingredient is any skinned split pulse, including lentils, and in India there is a distinction made between these and *gram*, whole pulses. Dal is also the name applied to the main course or side dish made from these pulses, served always with rice or breads such as chapatis or *naan*, the cereal supplying the missing elements to what would be, on its own, an incomplete protein.

Often neglected in other countries, the many varieties of pulses in India are turned into literally hundreds of different dishes. In the South, dal dishes tend to have a soup-like consistency, such as the very spicy *sambhar*, whereas in the North they are more likely to be thickened stews. Much of a dal's flavour is provided by the finishing touch, the *tarka*, a few spices tempered in hot oil, which is then poured over the cooked pulses to bring the dish alive.

250 g (1 cup) sabat urad
   (whole black gram/black lentil)
1 onion, roughly chopped
2 garlic cloves, roughly chopped
5 cm (2 in) piece of ginger,
   roughly chopped
1 green chilli, roughly chopped
120 ml (½ cup) oil
2 tablespoons ground cumin
1 tablespoon ground coriander
2 teaspoons salt
¼ teaspoon chilli powder
3 tablespoons garam masala (page 251)
150 ml (⅔ cup) cream

Serves 6

Put the whole black gram in a large, heavy-based saucepan, add 2 litres
(8 cups) water and bring to the boil. Reduce the heat and simmer for 1 hour,
or until the dal feels soft when pressed between the thumb and index finger.
Most of the dal will split to reveal the creamy insides. Drain the gram,
reserving the cooking liquid.

Blend the onion, garlic, ginger and chilli together in a food processor to form
a paste, or finely chop them together with a knife. Heat the oil in a frying
pan and fry the onion mixture over high heat, stirring constantly, until golden
brown. Add the cumin and coriander and fry for 2 minutes. Add the dal and
stir in the salt, chilli powder and garam masala. Pour 300 ml (1¼ cups) of
the reserved dal liquid into the pan, bring to the boil, then reduce the heat
and simmer for 10 minutes. Just before serving, stir in the cream and simmer
for another 2 minutes to heat through.

kali dal

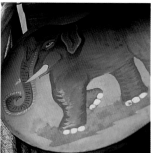

chole chaat

225 g (8 oz) chickpeas
2 tablespoons oil
½ onion, chopped
1 teaspoon ground coriander
1 teaspoon ground cumin
¼ teaspoon ground turmeric
1 teaspoon garam masala (page 251)
2 cm (¾ in) piece of ginger, grated
2 red chillies, finely chopped
200 g (7 oz) tin chopped tomatoes,
   drained

Serves 4

Soak the chickpeas overnight in 2 litres (8 cups) of water. Drain, then put the chickpeas in a large saucepan with another 2 litres (8 cups) water. Bring to the boil, spooning off any scum from the surface, then simmer over low heat for 1–1½ hours, until soft. It is important the chickpeas are soft at this stage as they won't soften any more once the sauce has been added. Drain the chickpeas, reserving the cooking liquid. Remove ½ cup of the chickpeas and thoroughly mash them with a fork.

Heat the oil in a heavy-based saucepan over low heat and cook the onion until golden. Add the coriander, cumin, turmeric and garam masala and fry for 1 minute. Add the ginger, chilli, tomato and salt, to taste, and stir until mixed. Add the chickpeas and their cooking liquid, and the mashed chickpeas. Bring to the boil, reduce the heat and simmer, uncovered, for 5 minutes.

**50 g (½ cup) moong dal
   (yellow mung beans)**
**200 g (7 oz) carrots or white radish,
   finely grated**
25 g (½ cup) grated coconut
25 g (¾ cup) coriander (cilantro) leaves
½ tablespoon oil
½ teaspoon yellow mustard seeds
2 dried chillies
2 tablespoons lemon juice

Serves 4

Soak the dal in plenty of boiling water for 3 hours, then drain.

Combine the dal, carrot, coconut and the coriander leaves in a salad bowl. Heat the oil in a small saucepan over medium heat, add the mustard seeds, then cover and shake the pan until the seeds start to pop. Add the chillies, remove from the heat and add the lemon juice. When cold, pour over the remaining ingredients and toss well. Season with salt, to taste.

kosambri

lemon pickle

500 g (1 lb 2 oz) thin-skinned lemons
½ teaspoon ground turmeric
2 tablespoons salt
½ teaspoon fenugreek seeds
1 teaspoon yellow mustard seeds
½ tablespoon chilli powder
2 tablespoons oil

Makes 500 ml (2 cups)

Wash the lemons, place them in a saucepan with 500 ml (2 cups) water and the turmeric and bring slowly to the boil, skimming off any scum which rises to the top. Boil for 8 minutes, then remove from the heat and drain well.

Cut each lemon into eight sections and remove any pips. By this time, the lemon flesh will have turned to a pulp. Sprinkle the lemons with the salt and pack them into a 500 ml (2-cup) glass jar which has been sterilized (wash the jar in boiling water and dry in a warm oven). Put the lid on tightly and keep the lemons in the jar for 1 week, turning the jar over every day. If the lid of the jar is too narrow to balance upside down, store the jar on its side and roll it over every day instead.

Place a small frying pan over low heat and dry-roast the fenugreek and mustard seeds until aromatic and starting to pop, shaking the pan occasionally to prevent them from burning. Grind the roasted seeds to a fine powder using a spice grinder or mortar and pestle.

Tip the lemons into a bowl and mix in the ground spices and the chilli powder. Clean the jar and sterilize it again. Put the lemons and any juices back into the jar and pour the oil over the top to act as an air barrier and stop the top layer from discolouring. Store in a cool place, or in the fridge after opening.

1 tablespoon oil
2 garlic cloves, crushed
1 teaspoon grated ginger
2 cinnamon sticks
4 cloves
½ teaspoon chilli powder
1 kg (2 lb 4 oz) fresh or frozen ripe mango
   flesh, roughly chopped
375 ml (1½ cups) clear vinegar
250 g (1 cup) caster (superfine) sugar

Makes 500 ml (2 cups)

Heat the oil in a heavy-based saucepan over medium heat, add the garlic and ginger and fry for 1 minute. Add the remaining ingredients and bring to the boil.

Reduce the heat to low and cook for 1 hour, or until the mango is thick and pulpy, like jam. It should fall in sheets off the spoon when it is ready. Add salt, to taste, and more chilli if you wish. Remove the whole spices.

Pour the chutney into hot sterilized jars (wash the jars in boiling water and dry them thoroughly in a warm oven). Seal the jars and allow to cool completely. Store in a cool place, or in the fridge after opening.

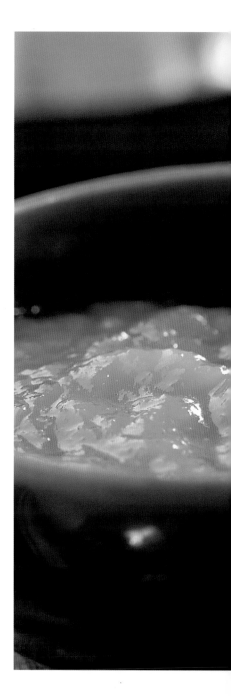

mango chutney

chutney...

Chutneys, pickles and relishes are never left on the side of the Indian plate. An essential part of the meal, they are practically considered dishes in their own right, a cheap lunch perhaps consisting of little more than a delicious homemade chutney and pile of fresh *roti* (bread). A spoonful of chutney is a way of pepping up the appetite on the hottest days, and a tiny bite lends a refreshing taste to a savoury dish. In India, a chutney is chosen for its ability to add sweet, sour, salty and hot tastes to a meal.

There is a gulf of difference between the sweet chutneys of the West and the pungent *chatni* of India. The Indian *chatni*, from which the English 'chutney' is taken, is a hot raw sauce, sometimes bottled, but more usually made fresh from a combination of green chillies, handfuls of vibrant coriander and mint, ginger, garlic and onion, sometimes with the addition of coconut, tamarind or fruit. This sour and piquant relish is an important Indian taste, and one that enlivens blander food such as rice, vegetables and dal. Chutneys are served in small, non-metallic bowls. Coconut chutney is a symbol of the South, fresh mint chutney an indispensable part of a northern meal of *tandoori* meats and breads. The Western chutney, despite often being made in India, is more sweet than sweet-and-sour, a cooked combination of sugar, vinegar, spices and fruit that is really more of a pickle than a true chutney.

Pickles, *achar*, are preserves of fruit and vegetables held in vinegar, brine or, in the case of lemons and limes, in their own juice. In a hot country, pickling has long been the best way of extending the storage life of fresh food, and the Indians make many, including fish and meat pickles. Many pickles are hot, though they may also be sour, sweet, or a mixture of all three flavours.

The Indians have a passion for tempting accompaniments served with their meals and, besides pickles and chutneys, the Indian cook makes many relishes. At its most simple, a relish can be a chopped red onion, chunks of green chilli or ripe fruit. It can also be something more: refreshing tomato and cucumber sprinkled with lime juice and spices, or a pot of *raita* — iced yoghurt and vegetables.

yoghurt rice

**2 tablespoons urad dal
(black gram/black lentils)
2 tablespoons chana dal (gram lentils)
225 g (1 cup) basmati rice
2 tablespoons oil
½ teaspoon mustard seeds
12 curry leaves
3 dried chillies
¼ teaspoon ground turmeric
pinch of asafoetida
500 ml (2 cups) thick plain yoghurt
or recipe page 250**

Serves 4

Soak the dals in 250 ml (1 cup) boiling water for 3 hours. Wash the rice in a sieve under cold running water until the water from the rice runs clear. Drain.

Put the rice and 500 ml (2 cups) water in á saucepan and bring rapidly to the boil. Stir, cover, reduce the heat to a slow simmer and cook for 10 minutes. Leave for 15 minutes before fluffing up with a fork.

Drain the dals and pat dry with paper towels. For the final seasoning (*tarka*), heat the oil in a small saucepan over low heat, add the mustard seeds, cover and shake the pan until the seeds start to pop. Add the curry leaves, chillies and the dals and fry for 2 minutes, stirring occasionally. Stir in the turmeric and asafoetida.

Put the yoghurt in a large bowl, pour the fried dal mixture into the yoghurt and mix thoroughly. Mix the rice into the spicy yoghurt. Season with salt, to taste. Cover and refrigerate. Serve cold but, before serving, stand the rice at room temperature for about 10 minutes. Serve as part of a meal. Yoghurt rice goes very well with meat dishes.

60 g (¼ cup) toor dal (yellow lentils)
300 g (1½ cups) basmati rice
3 tablespoons ghee
1 teaspoon cumin seeds
6 cloves
½ cinnamon stick
2 onions, finely chopped
2 garlic cloves, finely chopped
2 cm (¾ in) piece of ginger, finely chopped
1 teaspoon garam masala (page 251)
3 tablespoons lemon juice
1 teaspoon salt

Serves 6

Soak the dal in 500 ml (2 cups) water in a large saucepan for 2 hours. Wash the rice in a sieve under cold water until the water from the rice runs clear. Drain.

Heat the ghee in a heavy-based saucepan over low heat and fry the cumin seeds, cloves and cinnamon for a few seconds. Increase the heat to medium, add the onion, garlic and ginger and cook until they soften and begin to brown.

Add the rice and dal and toss to thoroughly coat in ghee. Add the garam masala, lemon juice, salt and 750 ml (3 cups) boiling water. Bring to the boil, then reduce the heat to very low, cover and cook for 15 minutes. Remove from the heat and gently fluff up with a fork. Cover the pan with a clean cloth and leave for 10 minutes. Fluff up again and season with salt, to taste.

khichhari

chapatis

200 g (1⅓ cups) atta (chapati flour) or
100 g (⅔ cup) wholemeal flour and
100 g (¾ cup) plain (all-purpose flour)
½ teaspoon salt
100 g (4 oz) ghee or clarified butter

Makes 8

Sift the atta and salt into a bowl and make a well in the centre. Add about 150 ml (⅔ cup) tepid water, enough to mix to form a soft, pliable dough. Turn the dough out onto a floured work surface and knead for 5 minutes. Place in an oiled bowl, cover and allow to rest for 30 minutes.

Put a *tava* or griddle, or a heavy-based frying pan over medium heat and leave it to heat up. Divide the dough into eight equal portions. Working with one portion at a time and keeping the rest covered, on a lightly floured surface roll out each portion to form a circle with a 15 cm (6 in) diameter. Keep the rolled chapatis covered with a damp cloth while you roll them and cook them. Remove the excess surface flour on the chapati prior to cooking by holding the chapati in the palms of your hands and gently slapping it from one hand to the other. If you leave the flour on it may burn.

Place each chapati on the *tava*, leave it for 7–10 seconds to brown, then turn it over to brown on the other side. Depending on the hotness of the *tava*, the second side should take about 15 seconds. Turn over the chapati again and, using a folded tea towel, apply gentle pressure to the chapati in several places to heat it and encourage it to puff up like a balloon. It is this puffing-up process that gives the chapati its light texture. Smear the hot chapati with a little of the ghee, and leave stacked and covered with a tea towel until all the chapatis are cooked.

**200 g (½ bunch) English spinach leaves,
   stalks removed**
**500 g (3⅔ cups) atta (chapati flour) or
   250 g (1⅔ cups) wholemeal flour and
   250 g (2 cups) plain (all-purpose) flour**
1 teaspoon salt
1 teaspoon ghee or oil
ghee or oil, for cooking

Makes 20

Cook the spinach briefly in a little simmering water until it is just wilted, then refresh in cold water. Drain thoroughly, then finely chop. Squeeze out any extra water by putting the spinach between two plates and pushing them together.

Sift the atta and salt into a bowl and make a well in the centre. Add the spinach, ghee and about 250 ml (1 cup) tepid water and mix to form a soft, pliable dough. Turn out the dough onto a floured work surface and knead for 5 minutes. Place in an oiled bowl, cover and allow to rest for 30 minutes.

Divide the dough into 20 balls. Working with one portion at a time and keeping the rest covered, on a lightly floured surface roll out each portion evenly to a 12 cm (5 in) circle about 1 mm (¹∕₁₂ in) thick.

Heat a *tava*, griddle or heavy-based frying pan until hot, oil it with ghee and cook one roti at a time. Cook each on one side, covered with a saucepan lid (this will help keep them soft), for about 1 minute. Turn it over, cover again and cook the other side for 2 minutes. Check the roti a few times to make sure it doesn't overcook. The roti will blister a little and brown in some places. Remove the roti and keep it warm under a tea towel. Cook the remaining *roti*.

saag roti

a little taste of...

Tandoori food is rarely eaten in Indian homes, few families possessing any oven, let alone the fiercely hot clay *tandoor* oven needed to create the cuisine's earthy flavour. The tandoor has its origins in the Middle East, but in India it is associated with the Punjabi countryside, where community ovens were used to roast meats and bake breads. Tandoori is now India's best-known cuisine, largely because it was mainly the Punjabis who created the Indian restaurant menu. The secret of the tandoor is its heat, which singes the food yet cooks it so quickly that it doesn't dry out. Additional flavour comes from a marinade of cumin, coriander, ginger, chilli and turmeric stirred into meat-tenderizing yoghurt, the orange colour usually a result of red food colouring. Threaded onto long skewers, chunks of meat, *tikka*, and whole chickens are fed through the top of the oven to stand upright, while *naan* breads are slapped onto the sides, puffing up within a minute. Accompaniments are kept simple: onion rings, lime wedges and cucumber and tomato slices with a mint and coriander chutney.

...tandoor

tandoori chicken

1.5 kg (3 lb 5oz) chicken or skinless
   chicken thighs and drumsticks

MARINADE
2 teaspoons coriander seeds
1 teaspoon cumin seeds
1 onion, roughly chopped
3 garlic cloves, roughly chopped
5 cm (2 in) piece of ginger, roughly
   chopped
250 ml (1 cup) thick plain yoghurt
   or recipe page 250
grated rind of 1 lemon

3 tablespoons lemon juice
2 tablespoons clear vinegar
1 teaspoon paprika
2 teaspoons garam masala (page 251)
½ teaspoon tandoori food colouring
   (optional)

2 tablespoons ghee
onion rings
lemon wedges

Serves 4

Remove the skin from the chicken and cut the chicken in half. Using a sharp knife, make diagonal incisions, 2.5 cm (1 in) long, on each limb and breast, taking care not to cut through to the bone. If using thighs and drumsticks, trim away any excess fat and make an incision in each piece.

To make the marinade, place a frying pan over low heat and dry-roast the coriander seeds until aromatic. Remove and dry-roast the cumin seeds. Grind the roasted seeds to a fine powder using a spice grinder or mortar and pestle. In a food processor, blend the marinade ingredients to form a smooth paste or finely chop the onion, garlic and ginger with a knife and mix with the rest of the ingredients in a bowl. Season with salt, to taste. Marinate the chicken for at least 8 hours, or overnight. Turn the chicken occasionally to soak all sides.

Heat the oven to 200°C (400°F/Gas 6). Place the chicken on a wire rack on a baking tray. Cover with foil and roast on the top shelf for 45–50 minutes or until cooked through (test by inserting a skewer into a thigh; the juices should run clear). Baste the chicken with the marinade once during cooking. Remove the foil 15 minutes before the end of cooking, to brown the tandoori mixture. Preheat the grill (broiler) to its highest setting.

Prior to serving, while the chicken is still on the rack, heat the ghee, pour it over the chicken halves and cook under the grill for 5 minutes to blacken the edges of the chicken as would happen in a tandoor. Serve the chicken garnished with onion rings and lemon wedges. The chicken pieces can also be grilled, barbecued or spit-roasted.

MARINADE
500 ml (2 cups) thick plain yoghurt
    or recipe page 250
½ onion, finely chopped
2 cm (¾ in) piece of ginger, grated
4 garlic cloves, crushed
1 teaspoon ground coriander
2 tablespoons lemon juice
1½ tablespoons garam masala (page 251)
1 teaspoon paprika
1 teaspoon chilli powder
2 tablespoons tomato purée
1 teaspoon salt

500 g (1 lb 2 oz) skinless firm white fish
    such as halibut, monkfish or blue-eye
2 onions, each cut into 8 chunks
2 small green or red capsicum (peppers),
    each cut into 8 chunks

50 g (2 oz) cucumber, peeled and diced
1 tablespoon chopped coriander (cilantro)
lemon wedges

Serves 8

To make the marinade, mix half the yoghurt with all the other marinade ingredients in a shallow dish that is long enough and deep enough to take the prepared skewers. You will need eight metal skewers.

Cut the fish into about 24–32 bite-size chunks. On each metal skewer, thread three or four pieces of fish and chunks of onion and pepper, alternating them as you go. Put the skewers in the marinade and turn them so that all the fish and vegetables are well coated. Cover and marinate in the fridge for at least 1 hour, or until you are ready to cook.

Preheat the barbecue or grill (broiler). Lift the skewers out of the marinade. Cook on the barbecue, or under a grill on a wire rack set above a baking tray, for 5–6 minutes, turning once, or until the fish is cooked and firm and both the fish and the vegetables are slightly charred.

Meanwhile, stir the cucumber and coriander into the other half of the yoghurt. Serve the fish with the yoghurt and lemon wedges.

fish tikka

tandoori paneer

300 g (11 oz) paneer (page 249)
2 green capsicum (peppers)
1 onion
2 firm tomatoes
300 ml (1¼ cups) thick plain yoghurt
   or recipe page 250
1 teaspoon ground turmeric
2 cm (¾ in) piece of ginger, grated
4 garlic cloves, crushed
1½ tablespoons lemon juice
2 tablespoons chopped mint leaves
1 tablespoon chopped coriander
   (cilantro) leaves
2 tablespoons oil

Serves 4

Cut the paneer into pieces measuring about 2 x 1.5 cm (2 x ½ in). Cut the capsicum into squares, the onion into chunks and the tomatoes into cubes. Mix the yoghurt, turmeric, ginger, garlic and lemon juice, together with a little salt, in a large bowl. Stir in the herbs. Add the paneer and vegetables to the marinade, cover and refrigerate for 3 hours.

Preheat the grill (broiler) to its highest setting. Using eight skewers, thread onto each five pieces of paneer and some capsicum, onion and tomato, dividing the vegetables equally. Brush with the oil, season with salt and grill on all sides for 3–4 minutes, or until the paneer and vegetables are cooked and slightly charred around the edges. Serve with roti (saag roti, page 146) and a salad such as laccha (page 166).

MARINADE
½ tablespoon paprika
1 teaspoon chilli powder
2 tablespoons garam masala (page 251)
¼ teaspoon tandoori food colouring
1½ tablespoons lemon juice
4 garlic cloves, roughly chopped
5 cm (2 in) piece of ginger,
    roughly chopped
15 g (½ cup) coriander (cilantro) leaves,
    chopped
100 ml (½ cup) thick plain yoghurt
    or recipe page 250

500 g (1 lb 2 oz) skinless chicken breast
    fillets, cut into 2.5 cm (1 in) cubes
wedges of lemon

Serves 4

For the marinade, blend all the ingredients together in a food processor until smooth, or finely chop the garlic, ginger and coriander leaves with a knife and mix with the rest of the marinade ingredients. Season with salt, to taste.

Put the chicken cubes in a bowl with the marinade and mix thoroughly. Cover and marinate overnight in the fridge.

Heat the oven to 200°C (400°F/Gas 6). Thread the chicken pieces onto four metal skewers and put them on a metal rack above a baking tray. Roast, uncovered, for 15–20 minutes, or until the chicken is cooked and browned around the edges. Serve with wedges of lemon to squeeze over the chicken.

chicken tikka

chicken
tikka masala

1 tablespoon oil
1 onion, finely chopped
2 cardamom pods
2 garlic cloves, crushed
400 g (14 oz) tin chopped tomatoes
¼ teaspoon ground cinnamon
1 tablespoon garam masala (page 251)
½ teaspoon chilli powder
1 teaspoon jaggery or soft brown sugar
300 ml (1¼ cups) cream
1 tablespoon ground almonds
1 quantity chicken tikka (page 158)
1 tablespoon chopped coriander
   (cilantro) leaves

Serves 6

Heat the oil in a *karhai* or heavy-based saucepan over low heat. Add the onion and cardamom pods and fry until the onion is soft and starting to brown. Add the garlic to the pan, cook for 1 minute, then add the tomato and cook until the paste is thick.

Add the cinnamon, garam masala, chilli powder and sugar to the pan and cook for 1 minute. Stir in the cream and almonds, then add the cooked chicken tikka pieces and gently simmer for 5 minutes, or until the chicken is heated through. Garnish with the chopped coriander.

500 g (4 cups) maida or plain
  (all-purpose) flour
300 ml (1¼ cups) milk
2 teaspoons (7 g/¼ oz) easy-blend
  dried yeast or 15 g (½ oz) fresh yeast
2 teaspoons kalonji (nigella seeds)
  (optional)
½ teaspoon baking powder

½ teaspoon salt
1 egg, beaten
2 tablespoons oil or ghee
200 ml (¾ cup) thick plain yoghurt
  or recipe page 250

Makes 10

Sift the maida into a large bowl and make a well in the centre. Warm the milk over low heat in a saucepan until it is hand-hot (the milk will feel the same temperature as your finger when you dip your finger into it). If you are using fresh yeast, mix it with a little milk and a pinch of maida and set it aside to activate and go frothy.

Add the yeast, kalonji, baking powder and salt to the maida. In another bowl, mix the egg, oil and yoghurt. Pour into the maida with 250 ml (1 cup) of the milk and mix to form a soft dough. If the dough seems dry add the remaining 50 ml (½ cup) of milk. Turn out onto a floured work surface and knead for 5 minutes, or until smooth and elastic. Put in an oiled bowl, cover and leave in a warm place to double in size. This will take several hours.

Preheat the oven to 200°C (400°F/Gas 6). Place a roasting tin half-filled with water at the bottom of the oven. This provides moisture in the oven which prevents the naan from drying out too quickly.

Punch down the dough, knead it briefly and divide it into 10 portions. Using the tips of your fingers, spread out one portion of dough to the shape of a naan bread. They are traditionally teardrop in shape, so pull the dough at one end. Put the naan on a greased baking tray. Bake on the top shelf for 7 minutes, then turn the naan over and cook for another 5 minutes. While the first naan is cooking, shape the next one. If your tray is big enough, you may be able to fit two at a time. Remove the cooked naan from the oven and cover with a cloth to keep it warm and soft.

Repeat the cooking process until all the dough is used. You can only use the top shelf of the oven because the naan won't cook properly on the middle shelf. Refill the baking tray with boiling water when necessary.

naan

roti

Although rice might seem curry's natural partner, for much of India's population, especially in the North, it is wheat that is the staple and bread the sustenance. The traditions behind Indian breadmaking are quite different from those in the West. Most Indian breads, *roti*, are unleavened flatbreads, a combination of just flour and water; they are the simplest types of breads to make. An absence of yeast can make breads heavy, but Indian flatbreads are rolled extremely thin, then cooked at searingly hot temperatures so air trapped during kneading lightens the dough, acting almost as a raising agent, the intense heat puffing up the bread.

Few Indian households own the oven needed to cook leavened breads, so instead, dough is cooked either on a heavy cast-iron griddle called a *tava* or, like puffed-up *puris*, deep-fried in a *karhai*, the Indian wok. An exception is the leavened bread *naan*, its charred smoky flavour a result of being cooked on the walls of a clay *tandoor* oven, and Hyderabad's *kulchas*, which are cooked in a similar way in a wood-fired oven. India's breads, from the most basic *chapati* to the flakiest *parathas*, are wielded with great expertise, torn up with just one hand, then used to scoop up meat and vegetables or dipped into liquidy curries.

laccha

1 red onion, finely sliced into rings
½ teaspoon salt
½ teaspoon cumin seeds
¼ teaspoon chilli powder
2 tomatoes, thinly sliced
450 g (1 lb) cucumbers, peeled
   and thinly sliced
3 tablespoons lemon juice

Serves 6

Mix the onion with the salt and leave in a sieve or colander to drain for 10 minutes. Rinse under cold water, then drain and put in a bowl.

Place a small frying pan over low heat and dry-roast the cumin seeds until aromatic. Grind the roasted seeds to a fine powder using a spice grinder or mortar and pestle. Add the cumin and chilli powder to the onion and mix well.

Arrange the tomato slices on a plate and top with a layer of cucumber, then onion. Sprinkle with the lemon juice and season with salt and black pepper, to taste.

450 g (1 lb) cucumber, grated
1 large, ripe tomato, finely chopped
300 ml (1¼ cups) thick plain yoghurt
  or recipe page 250
½ tablespoon oil
1 teaspoon black mustard seeds
1 tablespoon coriander (cilantro) leaves
  (optional)

Serves 4

Put the cucumber and tomato in a sieve for 20 minutes to drain off any excess liquid. Mix them in a bowl with the yoghurt and season with salt, to taste.

For the final seasoning (*tarka*), heat the oil in a small saucepan over medium heat, add the mustard seeds, then cover and shake the pan until the seeds start to pop. Pour the seeds and oil over the yoghurt. Serve sprinkled with the coriander leaves if you wish.

raita

a little taste of...

The kitchens of southern India have one indispensable ingredient, rice. Not only is a mound of steamed rice the accompaniment to every meal but it is also made into rice batters that are unique to the South. Crispy *dosas*, rice wraps, are eaten at breakfast or filled with spicy vegetables for a snack and *idlis*, spongy rice cakes, are delicious dipped into coconut chutney. The influence of the meat-loving Moghuls never reached the far South and, apart from the Christian communities of Goa and Kerala, this area has remained predominantly vegetarian. Two vegetable dishes appear at most meals: *sambhar*, a thin, fiery vegetable and dal stew, and *rasam*, a dal broth. The South is blessed with some of India's best seafood, and local fish cooked in a wet *masala*, spice mix, of bright green herbs, ginger and garlic, then simmered in fresh coconut milk, is one of the area's treats. Fresh herbs form the basis of most curries, and the addition of lots of chillies, sour tamarind or lime juice and curry leaves will mark any dish as unmistakably from the southern kitchen.

...southern kitchen

dosas

110 g (½ cup) urad dal
  (black gram/black lentils)
1 teaspoon salt
300 g (1¾ cups) rice flour
oil, for cooking

Makes 20

Put the dal in a medium bowl and cover with water. Soak for at least 4 hours or overnight.

Drain, then grind the dal with the salt and a little water in a food processor or blender, or use a mortar and pestle, to form a fine paste. Mix the paste with the rice flour, add 1 litre (4 cups) water and mix well. Cover with a cloth and leave in a warm place for 8 hours, or until the batter ferments and bubbles. The batter will double in volume.

Heat a *tava* or a non-stick frying pan over medium heat and leave to heat up. Don't overheat it; the heat should always be medium. Lightly brush the surface of the tava or frying pan with oil. Stir the batter and pour a ladleful into the middle of the griddle and quickly spread it out with the back of the ladle or a palette knife, to form a thin pancake. Don't worry if the dosa is not perfect—they are very hard to get exactly right. Drizzle a little oil around the edge to help it become crisp. Cook until small holes appear on the surface and the edges start to curl. Turn over with a spatula and cook the other side. (The first dosa is often a disaster but it will season the pan for the following ones.)

Repeat with the remaining mixture, oiling the pan between each dosa. Roll the dosas into big tubes and keep warm. Dosas are often filled with potato masala filling (page 174) and served with sambhar (page 178) and chutneys, or with curries.

2 tablespoons oil
1 teaspoon black mustard seeds
10 curry leaves
¼ teaspoon ground turmeric
1 cm (¼ in) piece of ginger, grated
2 green chillies, finely chopped
2 onions, chopped
500 g (1 lb 2 oz) waxy potatoes,
** cut into 2 cm (¾ in) cubes**
1 tablespoon tamarind purée (page 250)

Serves 4

Heat the oil in a heavy-based frying pan, add the mustard seeds, cover and, when they start to pop, add the curry leaves, turmeric, ginger, chilli and onion and cook, uncovered, until the onion is soft.

Add the potato cubes and 250 ml (1 cup) water to the pan, bring to the boil, cover and cook until the potato is tender and almost breaking up. If there is any liquid left in the pan, simmer, uncovered, until it evaporates. If the potato isn't cooked and there is no liquid left, add a little more and continue to cook. Add the tamarind purée and season with salt, to taste.

potato masala

idlis

220 g (1 cup) **urad dal**
  (black gram/black lentils)
100 g (½ cup) **rice flour**
1 teaspoon **fenugreek seeds**
1 teaspoon **salt**

Makes 20

Put the the dal in a large bowl, cover with water and soak for at least 4 hours, or overnight.

Drain the dal, then grind in a food processor or blender or use a mortar and pestle with a little water, to form a fine paste.

Combine the rice flour, fenugreek seeds and salt in a large bowl and mix in enough water to make a thick, pourable batter. Mix the batters together. Cover with a cloth and leave in a warm place for 8 hours, until the batter ferments and bubbles. The batter will double in volume.

Pour the mixture into a greased idli mould, filling the cups to almost full. Cover and steam the idlis over simmering water for 10–15 minutes, until they are firm and puffed. Traditionally, the idlis are eaten with sambhar (page 178) or as an accompaniment for dishes that have plenty of sauce.

225 g (¾ cup) toor dal (yellow lentils)
2 tablespoons coriander seeds
10 black peppercorns
½ teaspoon fenugreek seeds
2 tablespoons grated coconut
1 tablespoon roasted chana dal
   (gram lentils)
6 dried chillies
2 drumstick vegetables (sahjan),
   cut into 5 cm (2 in) pieces
2 carrots, cubed

1 onion, roughly chopped
125 g (5 oz) eggplant (aubergine), cubed
50 g (2 oz) small okra, topped and tailed
1 tablespoon tamarind purée (page 250)
2 tablespoons oil
1 teaspoon black mustard seeds
10 curry leaves
½ teaspoon ground turmeric
½ teaspoon asafoetida

Serves 6

Soak the dal in 500 ml (2 cups) water for 2 hours. Drain the dal and put them in a saucepan with 1 litre (4 cups) of water. Bring to the boil, then skim off any scum from the surface. Cover and simmer for 2 hours, or until the dal is cooked and tender.

Place a small frying pan over low heat and dry-roast the coriander, peppercorns, fenugreek, coconut, chana dal and chillies, stirring constantly until the coconut is golden brown. Grind the roasted mixture to a fine powder using a mortar and pestle or a spice grinder.

Bring 750 ml (3 cups) water to the boil in a saucepan. Add the pieces of drumstick and the cubed carrot and bring back to the boil. Simmer for 10 minutes, then add the onion, eggplant and okra and more water if necessary. Simmer until the vegetables are almost cooked.

Put the boiled dal and their liquid, the ground spices, the vegetables (with any vegetable water) and tamarind in a large saucepan and bring slowly to the boil. Reduce the heat and simmer for 30 minutes. Season with salt, to taste.

Heat the oil in a small saucepan over medium heat, add the mustard seeds, cover and shake the pan until they start to pop. Add the curry leaves, turmeric, asafoetida and a little salt. Pour onto the simmering dal and stir until well mixed

sambhar

chillies... It is hard to imagine Indian food before the Portuguese arrived in the South with their prized New World discovery, the chilli. Few ingredients can shape a cuisine the way chillies can, and the Indians, already used to cooking with an array of spices, adopted the chilli pepper as their own. The plant flourished in the hot, steamy climate and India is now the world's largest chilli producer with hundreds of varieties, ranging from mild, bright red Kashmiri chillies to the tiny, searingly hot *dhani*, bird's-eye chillies.

For many of the world's poorest people, the chillis are a cheap way of making bland dishes more palatable, but in Indian cookery they are never used indiscriminately. Many Indian dishes, especially those of the North, contain very

little chilli at all, relying instead on complex blends of spices for flavour. Where a dish does call for chillies, they are added in a subtle and sophisticated way, contributing not just heat, but colour, aroma and flavour as well.

The foundation for almost every Indian curry is the *masala*, a spice paste that usually includes unripe, fresh green chillies, garlic, ginger and spices. Dried or powdered red chillies, which are rarely used fresh in Indian cooking, are added later, often as part of the *tarka*, a final seasoning of chilli, mustard seeds and curry leaves, fried in oil, then stirred into a dish just before serving.

Chillies are never allowed to overpower the rich layers of flavour built up in the *masala*, even in the fiery cooking of the South where chillies are valued for their power to cool the body down. The Indian cook must also take into account a chilli's unique taste, recognizing that a local variety is often vital to the distinctive character of a regional dish. Each carefully constructed curry is served as part of a balanced Indian meal, where dishes of different heats, usually only one very hot, are combined with a cooling *raita* or curds and a hot pickle or often a fresh chilli chutney.

masala vada

100 g (½ cup) urad dal
   (black gram/black lentils)
120 g (¾ cup) chana dal (gram lentils)
2 green chillies, seeded and finely chopped
8 curry leaves, roughly chopped
½ teaspoon fennel seeds, crushed
1 red onion, finely chopped
½ teaspoon garam masala (page 251)
3 tablespoons grated coconut
3 cm (1 in) piece of ginger, grated
4 tablespoons chopped coriander
   (cilantro) leaves
3 tablespoons rice flour or urad dal flour
pinch of baking powder (optional)
oil, for deep-frying

Makes 18

Soak the dal in cold water for 4 hours, then drain. Reserve 2 tablespoons of the soaked dal and coarsely grind the remainder in a food processor or use a mortar and pestle. Add the reserved dal to the ground dal for texture. Add the chopped chillies, curry leaves, fennel, onion, garam masala, coconut, ginger and coriander leaves. Mix well and season with salt. Add the flour and baking powder, if using (it gives a crisper texture), then mix until the texture is soft but the dough can be shaped (you may need to add a little water). Divide the mixture into 18 portions and form each into a ball. Slightly flatten each ball to form a patty.

Fill a *karhai* or heavy-based saucepan to one-third full with oil and heat to 180°C (350°F/Gas 4) or until a cube of bread fries brown in 15 seconds when dropped in the oil. Fry the patties in the hot oil, in batches of four or five, until golden brown and crisp. Drain well on paper towels and serve hot with a chutney.

½ teaspoon ground turmeric
200 g (7 oz) carrots, cut into batons
200 g (7 oz) sweet potato, cut into batons
200 g (7 oz) green beans, topped and
   tailed and cut in half
50 g (¾ cup) grated coconut
5 cm (2 in) piece of ginger, grated
3 green chillies, finely chopped
1½ teaspoons ground cumin
400 ml (1¾ cups) thick plain yoghurt
   or recipe page 250
1 tablespoon oil
10 curry leaves

Serves 4

Bring 500 ml (2 cups) water to the boil in a saucepan, add the turmeric and carrot, reduce the heat and simmer for 5 minutes. Add the sweet potato and the beans, return to the boil, then reduce the heat and simmer for another 5 minutes, or until the vegetables are almost cooked.

Put the coconut, ginger and chilli in a blender or use a mortar and pestle, with a little water, and blend or grind to a paste. Add to the vegetables with the cumin and some salt and simmer for 2 minutes. Stir in the yoghurt and heat through.

For the final seasoning (*tarka*), heat the oil over low heat in a small saucepan. Add the curry leaves and allow to crisp. Pour the hot oil and the curry leaves over the vegetables.

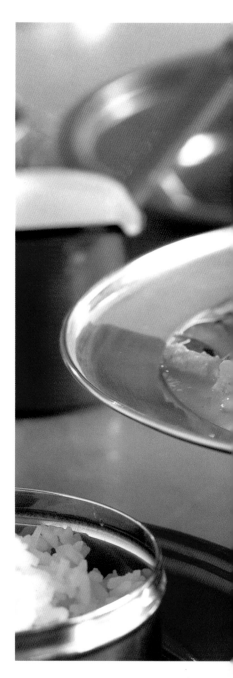

avial

prawns with
green mango

250 g (9 oz) tiger prawns
1½ teaspoons chilli powder
1 teaspoon ground turmeric
½ teaspoon cumin seeds
½ teaspoon yellow mustard seeds
4 garlic cloves, roughly chopped
4 cm (1½ in) piece of ginger,
**   roughly chopped**
1 red onion, roughly chopped
4 tablespoons oil
1 red onion, thinly sliced
1 green unripe mango, finely chopped

Serves 4

Peel and devein the prawns, leaving the tails intact. Put the chilli powder, turmeric, cumin, mustard, garlic, ginger and chopped red onion in a blender or food processor, or use a mortar and pestle, and process or grind to form a paste. If necessary, add a little water.

Heat the oil in a *karhai* or heavy-based frying pan and fry the sliced onion. When it starts to brown, add the curry paste and fry until aromatic.

Add the prawns and 200 ml (¾ cup) water to the pan, then cover and simmer for about 3–4 minutes, until the prawns are cooked and start to curl up. Add the mango and cook for another minute or two to thicken the curry. Season with salt, to taste.

SPICE MIX
6 dried chillies
1 tablespoon cumin seeds
1 teaspoon coriander seeds
1 teaspoon mustard seeds
¼ teaspoon garam masala (page 251)
½ teaspoon ground turmeric

3 tablespoons oil
1 onion, finely sliced
1 ripe tomato, chopped
2 onions, finely chopped
8 garlic cloves, chopped
6 green chillies, chopped
5 cm (2 in) piece of ginger, grated
100 ml (½ cup) tamarind purée
** (page 250)**
3 tablespoons coconut milk powder
** or coconut cream**
1 kg (2 lb 4 oz) salmon cutlets

Serves 6

Prepare the spice mix by grinding the chillies, cumin, coriander and mustard seeds to a fine powder using a spice grinder or mortar and pestle, then mixing with the garam masala and turmeric.

Heat the oil over low heat in a heavy-based frying pan large enough to hold the pieces of fish in a single layer. Add the sliced onion and fry until golden. Add the tomato, chopped onion, garlic, green chilli and ginger and fry, stirring occasionally, for 20 minutes, or until the oil separates from the sauce.

Add the spice mix and the tamarind purée to the pan, then bring to the boil. Add the coconut milk powder and stir until well mixed. Season with salt, to taste. Add the fish and bring slowly to the boil. The sauce is not very liquid but it needs to be made very hot in order to cook the fish. Simmer for 5 minutes, then turn the pieces of fish over and simmer for another 5 minutes, or until the fish is cooked through and the sauce is thick.

salmon curry

chilli crab

4 x 250 g (9 oz) small live crabs or
  2 x 500 g (1 lb 2 oz) live crabs
120 ml (½ cup) oil
2 garlic cloves, crushed
4 cm (1½ in) piece of ginger, grated
½ teaspoon ground cumin
½ teaspoon ground coriander
¼ teaspoon ground turmeric

¼ teaspoon cayenne pepper
1 tablespoon tamarind purée (page 250)
1 teaspoon sugar
2 small red chillies, finely chopped
2 tablespoons chopped coriander
  (cilantro) leaves

Serves 4

Put the crabs in the freezer for 2 hours to stun them. Using a large, heavy-bladed knife or cleaver, cut off the large front claws from each crab, then twist off the remaining claws.

Turn each body over and pull off each apron piece, then pull out the spongy grey gills and discard them. Cut each crab body in half (quarters if you are using the large crabs). Crack the large front claws with the handle of a cleaver or a rolling pin. Rinse off any chips of shell under cold running water and pat dry with paper towels.

Mix half the oil with the garlic, ginger, cumin, coriander, turmeric, pepper, tamarind, sugar, chilli and a pinch of salt until they form a paste. Heat the remaining oil in a *karhai* or large, deep, heavy-based frying pan over medium heat. Add the spice paste and stir for 30 seconds, or until aromatic.

Add the crab portions to the pan and cook, stirring constantly, for 2 minutes, making sure the spice mix gets rubbed into the cut edges of the crab. Add 50 ml (¼ cup) water, cover and steam the crabs, tossing them a couple of times during cooking, for another 5–6 minutes, or until cooked through. The crabs will turn pink or red when they are ready and the flesh will go opaque (make sure the large front claws are well cooked). Drizzle a little of the liquid from the pan over the crabs, scatter with the coriander leaves and serve.

1 tablespoon oil
1 large onion, thinly sliced
3 garlic cloves, crushed
2 small green chillies, finely chopped
2 teaspoons ground turmeric
1 teaspoon ground coriander
1 teaspoon ground cumin
4 cloves
6 curry leaves
400 ml (1¾ cups) coconut milk
½ teaspoon salt
600 g (1 lb 5 oz) pomfret, sole or
   leatherjacket fillets, skinned
1 tablespoon chopped coriander
   (cilantro) leaves
curry leaves

Serves 6

Heat the oil in a *karhai* or deep, heavy-based frying pan, add the onion and cook for 5 minutes. Add the garlic and chilli and cook for another 5 minutes, or until the onion has softened and looks translucent. Add the turmeric, coriander, cumin and cloves and stir-fry with the onion for 2 minutes. Stir in the curry leaves, coconut milk and salt and bring to just below boiling point. Reduce the heat and simmer for 20 minutes.

Cut each fish fillet into two or three large pieces and add them to the sauce. Bring the sauce back to a simmer and cook for 5 minutes, or until the fish is cooked through and flakes easily. Check the seasoning, add more salt if necessary, then stir in the coriander leaves. Garnish with the curry leaves.

molee

masala... The original Indian curry powders, *masalas* are spice blends that are the very essence of Indian cooking. A masala is an artfully crafted concoction, the spices ground fresh to retain their potency, the combination carefully considered so that no single spice overwhelms the dish. It would be unthinkable to an Indian cook to use the same masala for every curry, the unique blend of spices giving a dish its signature flavour. This need not necessarily be spicy, but can instead be aromatic and subtle; it all depends on the blender.

Almost every Indian dish starts out with a masala. The Indians do not add spices as they go, instead, the premixed masala is fried in a little oil, the heat necessary to release its aroma. Vegetables, pulses, meat or fish are then tossed and coated in the paste. In the North, masalas tend to be 'dry', any seeds dry-roasted, then pounded together with the remaining spices to form a powder. North Indian cooking would be unrecognizable without the most famous of all spice mixes, garam masala. This sharp mixture of cinnamon, cardamom, cloves, coriander, cumin and black pepper is the stamp of Moghul cuisine, preferred over chilli in the North to add a pungent kick to the region's food.

Garam masala is one of a handful of spice blends that are added at the end of cooking. Dry-roasted to bring out its flavour, it is sprinkled over robust, usually meat-based dishes, though sometimes added a little too freely at roadside stalls to make up for a lack of fresh spices. Other popular spice blends include *panch phoron*, an aromatic whole seed combination of cumin,

fennel, fenugreek, mustard and nigella seeds that gives Bengali vegetarian cooking its distinctive flavour, and black *goda masala*, ground from black spices such as pepper, cloves and cinnamon.

In the South, masalas are usually 'wet' combinations of fresh chillies, young ginger and handfuls of green herbs such as coriander or mint, ground together with lime juice, coconut or water, to form a paste. One popular dry masala is *sambhar podi*, a hot, spicy blend of dal, turmeric, coriander, cumin, pepper and fenugreek that is the distinctive taste of the vegetarian South.

rasam

3 tablespoons tamarind purée (page 250)
1½ tablespoons coriander seeds
2 tablespoons cumin seeds
1 tablespoon black peppercorns
1 tablespoon oil
5 garlic cloves, skins on, roughly pounded
1 red onion, thinly sliced
2–3 dried chillies, torn into pieces
2 stalks curry leaves
200 g (7 oz) skinless, boneless chicken
  thighs, cut into small pieces

Serves 4

Mix the tamarind purée with 750 ml (3 cups) water. Place a small frying pan over low heat and dry-roast the coriander seeds until aromatic. Remove, then dry-roast the cumin seeds, followed by the black peppercorns. Grind them together using a spice grinder or a mortar and pestle.

Heat the oil in a large, heavy-based saucepan over low heat, add the garlic and onion and fry until golden. Add the chilli and the curry leaves and fry for 2 minutes, or until they are aromatic. Add the tamarind water, the ground spices and season with salt. Bring to the boil, reduce the heat and simmer for 10 minutes.

Add the chicken to the saucepan with 250 ml (1 cup) water and simmer for 20 minutes, gradually adding another 250 ml (1 cup) water as the soup reduces. Remove any garlic skin which has floated to the top. Season with salt, to taste. Serve with rice (page 248).

oil, for deep-frying
1 potato, cut into small cubes
500 g (1 lb 2 oz) rump steak, thinly sliced
3 garlic cloves, crushed
1 teaspoon ground black pepper
1 tablespoon ginger juice (page 248)
2 tablespoons oil, extra
2 onions, sliced in rings
60 ml (¼ cup) beef stock
2 tablespoons tomato purée
½ tablespoon soy sauce
1 teaspoon chilli powder
3 tablespoons lemon juice
3 tomatoes, chopped
60 g (½ cup) fresh or frozen peas
coriander (cilantro) leaves (optional)

Serves 4

Fill a deep, heavy-based saucepan to one-third full with oil and heat to 180°C (350°F/Gas 4), or until a cube of bread fries brown in 15 seconds. Deep-fry the potato cubes until golden brown. Drain on paper towels.

Put the meat in a bowl, add the garlic, pepper and ginger juice and toss well. Heat the oil and fry the meat quickly in batches over high heat. Keep each batch warm as you remove it. Reduce the heat, fry the onion until golden, then remove.

Put the stock, tomato purée, soy sauce, chilli powder and lemon juice in the pan and cook over medium heat until reduced. Add the fried onion, cook for 3 minutes, add the chopped tomato and the peas, then stir well and cook for 1 minute. Add the beef and potato and toss well until heated through. Garnish with coriander leaves if you like.

fried beef kerala

pork vindaloo

1 kg (2 lb 4 oz) leg of pork on the bone
6 cardamom pods
1 teaspoon black peppercorns
4 dried chillies
1 teaspoon cloves
10 cm (4 in) piece of cinnamon stick, roughly broken
1 teaspoon cumin seeds
½ teaspoon ground turmeric
½ teaspoon coriander seeds
¼ teaspoon fenugreek seeds
4 tablespoons clear vinegar

1 tablespoon dark vinegar
4 tablespoons oil
2 onions, finely sliced
10 garlic cloves, finely sliced
5 cm (2 in) piece of ginger, cut into matchsticks
3 ripe tomatoes, roughly chopped
4 green chillies, chopped
1 teaspoon jaggery or soft brown sugar

Serves 4

Trim away any excess fat from the pork, remove the bone and cut the pork into 2.5 cm (1 in) cubes. Reserve the bone.

Split open the cardamom pods and remove the seeds. Finely grind the cardamom seeds, peppercorns, dried chillies, cloves, cinnamon stick, cumin seeds, turmeric, coriander seeds and fenugreek seeds in a spice grinder or use a mortar and pestle.

In a bowl, mix the ground spices together with the vinegars. Add the pork and mix thoroughly to coat well. Cover and marinate in the fridge for 3 hours.

Heat the oil in a *karhai* or heavy-based saucepan over low heat and fry the onion until lightly browned. Add the garlic, ginger, tomato and chilli and stir well. Add the pork, increase the heat to high and fry for 3–5 minutes, or until browned. Add 250 ml (1 cup) water and any of the marinade liquid left in the bowl, reduce the heat and bring slowly back to the boil. Add the jaggery and the pork bone. Cover and simmer for about 1½ hours, stirring occasionally until the meat is very tender. Discard the bone. Season with salt, to taste.

2 tablespoons chana dal (gram lentils)
4 tablespoons ghee or oil
75 g (½ cup) cashew nuts
1 teaspoon black mustard seeds
15 curry leaves
½ onion, finely chopped
140 g (1½ cups) coarse semolina
lime juice

Serves 4

Soak the dal in plenty of water for 3 hours. Drain, then put in a saucepan with 500 ml (2 cups) water. Bring to the boil and cook for 2 minutes. Drain the dal, then dry in a tea towel. Brush a little of the ghee onto the cashew nuts and toast them in a frying pan over low heat until they are golden.

Heat the remaining ghee in a heavy-based frying pan and add the mustard seeds and cooked dal. Cook until the seeds start to pop, then add the curry leaves and onion and cook until the onion softens. Add the semolina. Toss everything together and when the semolina is hot and the grains are brown and coated in oil, sprinkle with 500 ml (2 cups) boiling water, 100 ml (½ cup) at a time, tossing and stirring after each addition, until the water is absorbed. Season with salt, to taste. Sprinkle with lime juice and cashews.

upama

idiyappam

225 g (8 oz) rice sticks or vermicelli
4 tablespoons oil
50 g (⅓ cup) cashew nuts
½ onion, chopped
3 eggs
150 g (1 cup) fresh or frozen peas
10 curry leaves
2 carrots, grated
2 leeks, finely shredded
1 red capsicum (pepper), diced
2 tablespoons tomato sauce (ketchup)
1 tablespoon soy sauce
1 teaspoon salt

Serves 4

Soak the rice sticks in cold water for 30 minutes, then drain and put them in a saucepan of boiling water. Remove from the heat and leave in the pan for 3 minutes. Drain and refresh in cold water.

Heat 1 tablespoon oil in a frying pan and fry the cashews until golden. Remove, add the onion to the pan, fry until dark golden, then drain on paper towels. Cook the eggs in boiling water for 10 minutes to hard-boil, then cool them immediately in cold water. When cold, peel them and cut into wedges. Cook the peas in boiling water until tender.

Heat the remaining oil in a frying pan and briefly fry the curry leaves. Add the carrot, leek and capsicum and stir for 1 minute. Add the tomato sauce, soy sauce, salt and rice sticks and mix, stirring constantly to prevent the rice sticks from sticking to the pan. Serve on a platter and garnish with the peas, cashews, fried onion and egg wedges.

1 teaspoon chana dal (gram lentils)
1 teaspoon urad dal
  (black gram/black lentils)
½ fresh coconut, grated (160 g/1¾ cups)
2 green chillies, seeded and finely chopped
½ teaspoon salt
1 tablespoon oil
1 teaspoon black mustard seeds
5 curry leaves
1 teaspoon tamarind purée (page 250)

Serves 4

Soak the dals in cold water for 2 hours, then drain well.

Put the grated coconut, chilli and salt in a food processor and blend to a fine paste. If you don't have a food processor, either finely chop everything together with a knife or pound them in a mortar and pestle.

Heat the oil in a small saucepan and add the mustard seeds and dals, then cover and shake the pan until they start to pop. Add the curry leaves and fry for 1 minute, or until the dal browns. Add these ingredients to the coconut with the tamarind and mix well.

fresh coconut chutney

carrot pachadi

1 tablespoon oil
1 teaspoon black mustard seeds
2–3 dried chillies
¼ teaspoon asafoetida
1 stalk of curry leaves
600 ml (2½ cups) thick plain yoghurt
    or recipe page 250
4 carrots, finely grated
coriander (cilantro) leaves

Serves 4

Heat the oil in a small saucepan over medium heat, add the mustard seeds and chillies, then cover and shake the pan until the seeds start to pop. Remove from the heat and immediately stir in the asafoetida and curry leaves.

Whisk the yoghurt to remove any lumps, then mix in the grated carrot. Mix in the mustard seeds, chillies, asafoetida, curry leaves along with the oil, then season with salt, to taste. Garnish with coriander leaves.

2 small or 1 large pineapple, slightly green
1 teaspoon salt
1 red onion, thinly sliced into half rings
4 red chillies, seeded and finely chopped
4 garlic cloves, finely chopped
2 teaspoons ginger juice (page 248)
30 g (¼ cup) icing (confectioners') sugar,
 or to taste
6 tablespoons lime juice, or to taste

Serves 6

Peel the pineapple by cutting down the outside in strips. Remove any remaining eyes, then slice the pineapple lengthwise and remove the tough central core.

Rub the pineapple with the salt and leave it to sit for a few minutes in a colander to draw out some of the juices. Rinse, then chop into small chunks and drain well on paper towels.

Mix all the ingredients together in a bowl, adding enough sugar, lime juice, pepper and salt to achieve a balanced flavour. Chill and serve.

pineapple chutney

eggplant sambal

2 medium (about 500 g/1 lb 2oz)
   eggplants (aubergines)
½ tablespoon oil
½ teaspoon ground turmeric
3 tablespoons lime juice
2 red chillies, seeded and finely diced
1 small red onion, finely diced
4 tablespoons thick plain yoghurt
   or recipe page 250
coriander (cilantro) leaves

Serves 4

Preheat the oven to 200°C (400°F/Gas 6). Slice each eggplant in half and brush the cut halves with the oil and ground turmeric. Place the eggplants in a roasting tin and roast them for 30 minutes, or until they are browned all over and very soft.

Scoop the eggplant pulp into a bowl. Mash the pulp with the lime juice, chilli and onion, reserving some chilli and onion for garnish. Season with salt, to taste, then fold in the yoghurt. Garnish with the coriander leaves and remaining onion and chilli.

a little taste of...

The Indian *mithai*, or sweet, shop features a display of jewel-like food, comprising trays of pink, yellow and green sweets, studded with nuts or coated with gold or silver leaf. Mithai are usually bought as gifts for friends and relatives, and their rich, luxurious taste has also made them the food of the gods, served at every festive occasion. Most shoppers buy in bulk, packing an ornate gift box with their favourites, though many can't resist stopping to sample some of the shop's specialities, sitting at tables set up for just such snacking. The Indian sweet-making tradition is unique, based around rice and dairy products: thickened reduced milk, fudge, cheese or yoghurt, all soothing to the digestive system and packed with sugar and fat to keep them from spoiling in shops with no refrigeration. Indian sweets are so rich that they are more like a dessert, and in the sweet shop there is no distinction between the two: fudge-like squares of *barfi* and sweet pastries, *karanji*, are displayed alongside bowls of *rossogolas*, milk balls in syrup, and pots of *gajar halva*, carrot halva.

...the sweets shop

rossogollas

1 quantity chenna (page 249)
3 tablespoons chopped nuts (optional)

SYRUP
1 kg (4½ cups) sugar
3 tablespoons milk
rosewater (optional)

Serves 6

Divide the chenna dough into 30 portions and roll each into a ball. If you are using the nuts, make a hollow in each ball, add a few chopped nuts to the centre, then re-roll as a ball.

Make a thin syrup by combining the sugar with 1.5 litres (6 cups) of water in a heavy-based saucepan and simmering the mixture over low heat until it is slightly thickened. The syrup should feel sticky and greasy. Add the milk to the boiling syrup to clarify it; this will force any scum to rise to the surface. Skim off the scum with a spoon.

Drop the rossogollas into the clean boiling syrup, reduce the heat and simmer for 10 minutes, or until they float. Sprinkle a little water on the boiling syrup every 2 minutes to stop it reducing too much and foaming. When the rossogollas are cooked, they will float on the surface.

Remove from the heat and leave to cool in the syrup. If you would like a rose flavour, add a few drops of rosewater. Keep the rossogollas refrigerated until required. Serve with a little of the syrup poured over them.

**225 g (1¾ cups) maida or plain
(all-purpose) flour**
4 tablespoons oil or ghee
oil, for deep-frying

FILLING
10 cardamom pods
100 g (½ cup) sugar
5 cm (2 in) piece of cinnamon stick
150 g (1¾ cups) grated coconut

Makes 30

Sift the maida into a bowl. Add the oil and rub it in with your fingers until the mixture resembles breadcrumbs. Add 5 tablespoons warm water, a little at a time, and, using a palette knife, blend the dough together. Turn out onto a floured surface and knead for 5 minutes, until smooth and pliable. Cover and set aside for 15 minutes. Don't refrigerate or the oil will congeal.

To make the filling, remove the cardamom seeds from the pods and crush them using a spice grinder or mortar and pestle. In a heavy-based saucepan, combine the sugar, cinnamon and 200 ml (¾ cup) water. Heat until the sugar has dissolved. Bring to the boil, add the coconut, then stir over low heat until the liquid has evaporated and the mixture comes together. The mixture should not be dry. Remove from heat, add the cardamom and allow to cool.

On a lightly floured surface, roll out one-third of the pastry to make a circle with a 28 cm (11 in) diameter. Using an 8 cm (3 in) cutter, cut out 10 circles of pastry. Place ½ tablespoon of the filling in the centre of each circle, then moisten the edges with water. Seal into a semicircle and crimp the edge. Repeat until all the pastry and filling have been used. Cover until ready to fry.

Fill a *karhai* or deep, heavy-based saucepan to one-third full with oil and heat. Add a small piece of pastry and if it rises to the surface in a couple of seconds the oil is ready for use. Put in a few karanjis at a time and fry for 30–60 seconds, until lightly browned. Turn and brown them on the other side. Remove from the pan and place on a rack for 5 minutes before draining on paper towels. When cold, store in an airtight container for up to a week.

karanji

cashew nut barfi

500 g (3¼ cups) cashew nuts
6 cardamom pods
200 g (2 cups) powdered milk
2 tablespoons ghee or butter
¼ teaspoon ground cloves
200 g (1 cup) caster (superfine) sugar
2 sheets edible silver leaf (varak)
   (optional)

Serves 12

Place a frying pan over low heat and dry-roast the cashew nuts until browned. Cool and chop in a food processor or with a knife. Remove the cardamom seeds from the pods and crush them in a spice grinder or use a mortar and pestle. Line a 26 x 17 cm (10 x 7 in) baking tin with baking paper.

Combine the milk powder and cashew nuts in a large bowl and rub in the ghee until completely mixed in. Stir in the cardamom and cloves.

Combine the sugar and 250 ml (1 cup) water in a heavy-based saucepan and heat over low heat until the sugar melts. Bring to the boil and simmer for 5–7 minutes to make a sugar syrup. Quickly stir the sugar syrup into the cashew mixture — if you leave it too long it will stiffen — and spread the mixture into the baking tin (the mixture should be about 1.5 cm (½ in) thick). Smooth with a buttered spatula. Place the silver leaf on top by inverting the sheets onto the surface and peeling off the paper backing. Leave to cool, then slice into diamond shapes. Serve cold.

2 litres (8 cups) milk
10 cardamom pods, lightly crushed
6 tablespoons sugar
15 g (½ oz) almonds, blanched
  and finely chopped
15 g (½ oz) unsalted pistachio nuts,
  skinned and finely chopped
edible silver leaf (varak) (optional)

Makes 12

Put the milk and cardamom pods in a heavy-based saucepan and bring to the boil. Reduce the heat to low and simmer, stirring frequently, for about 2 hours, until the milk has reduced to a third of the original amount, about 750 ml (3 cups). Whenever a thin skin forms on top, stir it back in.

Add the sugar to the pan, simmer for 5 minutes, then strain into a shallow plastic freezer box. Add the almonds and half the pistachios, then cool. Put twelve 75 ml (⅓ cup) kulfi moulds or dariole moulds in the freezer to chill.

Place the kulfi mixture in the freezer and every 20 minutes, using electric beaters or a fork, give the ice-cream a good stir to break up the ice crystals. When the mixture is stiff, divide it among the moulds and freeze until hardened completely. Dip the moulds in hot water and turn out the kulfi. Sprinkle with the remaining pistachios and decorate with a piece of silver leaf.

kulfi

carrot halva

1 kg (2 lb 4 oz) carrots, coarsely grated
1 litre (4 cups) milk
100 g (4 oz) ghee
250 g (1 cup) caster (superfine) sugar
80 g (1 cup) raisins
1 teaspoon cardamom seeds, finely ground
50 g (½ cup) slivered almonds
ground cardamom

Serves 8

Put the grated carrot and milk in a heavy-based saucepan over low heat and bring to a simmer. Cook, stirring until the carrot is tender and the milk evaporates. This must be done slowly or the mixture will burn. Add the ghee and cook until the carrot starts to brown.

Add the sugar and cook until the mixture is thick and dry. Add the raisins, cardamom and almonds. Serve hot in small bowls, with cream or ice-cream, and sprinkle with a little ground cardamom.

SYRUP
450 g (2 cups) sugar
4–5 drops rosewater

GULAB JAMUN
100 g (1 cup) low-fat powdered milk
2 tablespoons self-raising flour
2 teaspoons fine semolina
2 tablespoons ghee
4 tablespoons milk, to mix
24 pistachio nuts (optional)
oil, for deep-frying

Makes 24

To make the syrup, put the sugar in a large heavy-based saucepan with 850 ml (3¾ cups) water. Stir over low heat to dissolve the sugar. Increase the heat and boil for 3 minutes to make a syrup. Stir in the rosewater and remove from the heat.

To make the gulab jamun, combine the powdered milk, flour, semolina and ghee in a bowl. Add enough milk to make a soft dough, mix until smooth, then divide into 24 portions. If using the pistachio nuts, press each piece of dough in the centre to make a hole, fill with a pistachio, then roll into a ball. If not using pistachios, just roll each piece into a ball.

Fill a *karhai* or deep saucepan to one-third full with oil. Heat the oil to 150°C (300°F/Gas 2), or until a cube of bread fries brown in 30 seconds. Fry the balls over low heat until golden brown all over. Remove with a slotted spoon and transfer to the syrup. When all the balls are in the syrup, bring the syrup to boiling point, then remove from the heat. Cool and serve the gulab jamun at room temperature.

gulab jamun

almond
sarbat

250 g (2½ cups) freshly ground almonds
1 kg (4½ cups) sugar
12 cardamom pods
almond essence, to taste
5–6 drops rosewater (optional)

Makes 250 ml (1 cup)

Put the almonds, sugar and 250 ml (1 cup) water in a large, heavy-based saucepan and cook over low heat, stirring constantly until the sugar dissolves. Grind the cardamom with 1 tablespoon water in a spice grinder or use a mortar and pestle. Add to the almond syrup. Stir the mixture, removing any scum from the top. Cook until the syrup thickens. Remove from the heat, strain through a sieve lined with muslin, and leave to cool.

Add the almond essence and rosewater, if using, and serve in long glasses, with water, over lots of crushed ice.

1 teaspoon cumin seeds
600 ml (2½ cups) thick plain yoghurt
  or recipe page 250
½ teaspoon salt

Serves 4

Place a small frying pan over low heat and dry-roast the cumin seeds until browned and aromatic.

Blend the roasted cumin seeds (reserve a few for garnish) with the yoghurt, salt and 300 ml (1¼ cups) water, either by hand or in a blender, and serve in tall glasses. If you would like the lassi a little colder, add about eight ice cubes to the blender, or stir them into the blended lassi. Garnish with the reserved cumin seeds.

salt lassi

sweets

The Indians aren't great dessert-eaters, most meals ending with fresh fruit, but this doesn't mean that they don't have a sweet tooth. Indian sweets, *mithai*, are legendary for their sweetness and these beautiful confections, shaped in wooden moulds or cloaked in gold and silver leaf, are a national obsession. However, unlike Western confectionery, sugar is rarely the major ingredient. Instead, most *mithai* are fashioned from milk, either boiled down to form a dough, *khoya*, or the curds separated out to make a sweetened *paneer*, *chenna*. To this the sweet-maker adds his flavourings, creating fudge-like coconut and pistachio *barfi*, creamy nut-filled slices, or deep-fried balls of *gulab jamun*, floating in a rose syrup.

Kolkata (Calcutta) is India's sweet-making capital, and Bengalis need no excuse to indulge in sweets, particularly the city's famous *rossogollas*, spongy milk balls. Elsewhere, numerous festivals and celebrations act as a catalyst for uninhibited sweet feasting. Divali, the festival of light, marks the time when sweet-production goes into frenzied overdrive, shops spilling out onto the streets to cope with panic-buying for family, friends, work colleagues and the gods.

mango lassi

500 g (1 lb 2oz) ripe mango
250 ml (1 cup) chilled milk
250 ml (1 cup) thick plain yoghurt
   or recipe page 250

Serves 4

Chop the mango to a pulp with a knife or in a blender, add a pinch of salt and push through a nylon sieve with the back of a spoon. Discard any fibres. The remaining syrup should be thick but should not contain any stringy bits of pulp. Refrigerate until cold.

Blend the mango with the milk and yoghurt, either by hand or in a blender. If you would like the lassi a little colder, add about eight ice cubes to the blender, or stir them into the blended lassi.

If you want to use green unripe mangoes, cook them with 250 g (1 cup) sugar and a little water and add 500 ml (2 cups) milk to the lassi, instead of yoghurt and milk.

500 ml (2 cups) milk
2 tablespoons sugar
2 cm (¾ in) piece of ginger
2 tablespoons freshly ground Keralan
   or other coffee
5 cardamom seeds, pounded
1 cinnamon stick
cocoa powder

Serves 4

Put the milk and sugar in a heavy-based saucepan, bring to the boil over low heat and keep at a low simmer.

Dry-roast the ginger under a grill (broiler) for 1 minute on each side, then pound in a mortar and pestle to crush it and release the juices. Add to the milk with the coffee, cardamom and cinnamon. Cover and allow the flavourings to steep in the heat for 3 minutes.

Strain off the dregs (the easiest way is to put the whole lot through a coffee plunger or very fine strainer), then pour the coffee from one jug to another in a steady stream. You need to hold the jugs far apart and repeat the process until the coffee begins to froth. Serve while still hot, garnished with a sprinkling of cocoa.

masala coffee

masala chai

2 cm (¾ in) piece of ginger
5 cm (2 in) piece of cinnamon stick
4 peppercorns
3 cloves
3 cardamom pods
1 tablespoon black Indian tea
250 ml (1 cup) milk
3 tablespoons sugar

Serves 6

Dry-roast the ginger under a grill (broiler) for 1 minute on each side. Put the ginger and spices in a spice grinder or use a mortar and pestle and roughly crush them. Put the spices, tea and milk in a saucepan with 1 litre (4 cups) water and bring to the boil. Leave for 3 minutes, then add the sugar, to taste.

Strain off the dregs (the easiest way is to put the whole lot through a coffee plunger or very fine strainer), then pour the tea from one jug to another in a steady stream. You need to hold the jugs far apart and repeat the process until the tea begins to froth. Serve while still hot, in glasses.

chai

'*Chai garam, garam chai*', 'hot tea, hot tea', is the call of the Indian railways, train journeys punctuated by vendors selling large cups of soothing, spicy, sweet tea. Though native to India, tea was reintroduced into the country from China in the 19th century, and a cup of 'cha' remains Britain and India's great shared love. India produces some of the world's finest tea, most notably delicate, aromatic Darjeeling, grown in the foothills of the Himalayas. But this is not the tea of India's roadside *chai-wallahs*, who construct a uniquely Indian brew from

low-grade black tea. The most usual method of brewing *chai* is simply to boil the tea, water, milk, sugar and *chai masala* (tea spices) all up together. The tea is strained, then poured from a height into a glass or beautiful hand-thrown clay cup to make the thick, milky tea frothy on top. This *masala chai* is usually flavoured with cardamom pods or cooling fresh ginger, though individual recipes might include other spices such as cinnamon, cloves and black pepper. It also includes lots of sugar, which is essential for bringing out the flavours of the spices.

basics

RICE

400 g (2 cups) basmati rice

Serves 6

Rinse the rice under cold running water until the water running away is clear, then drain well.

Put the rice in a heavy-based saucepan and add enough water to come about 5 cm (2 in) above the surface of the pan. (If you put your index finger into the rice so it rests on the bottom of the pan, the water will come up to the second joint.) Add 1 teaspoon of salt and bring the water quickly to the boil. When it boils, cover and reduce the heat to a simmer.

Cook for 15 minutes or until the rice is just tender, then remove the saucepan from the heat and rest the rice for 10 minutes without removing the lid. Fluff the rice with a fork before serving.

GINGER JUICE

5 cm (2 in) piece of ginger

Makes 2 tablespoons

Pound the ginger using a mortar and pestle, or grate with a fine grater into a bowl. Put the ginger into a piece of muslin, twist it up tightly and squeeze out all the juice.

PANEER

3 litres (12 cups) milk
6 tablespoons strained lemon juice,
or vinegar

CHENNA
1 teaspoon caster (superfine) sugar
1 teaspoon maida or plain
(all-purpose) flour

Makes 550 g (1 lb 4 oz)

To make the *paneer*, pour the milk into a large, heavy-based saucepan. Bring to the boil, stirring with a wooden spoon so the milk doesn't stick to the base of the pan. Reduce the heat and stir in the lemon juice, then heat over low heat for a few more seconds before turning the heat off as large bits of curd start to form. Shake the pan slowly to allow the curds to form and release the yellow whey.

If the curds are slow to form, put the pan over low heat again for a few seconds. This helps with the coagulation.

Line a colander with muslin or cheesecloth so that it overlaps the sides. Pour off the whey, gently collecting the curds in the colander. Carefully pull up the corners of the cheesecloth so it hangs like a bag, twist the cloth so the whey is released, then hold the 'bag' under running water to wash off the remaining whey, twisting some more to remove the excess liquid.

Leave the bag to hang from your tap for several hours so the weight of the curds releases more liquid and the cheese compacts. To remove more liquid, press the bag under a heavy weight, such as a tray with some tinned food piled on top, for about 1 hour. This will form a firm block of *paneer*. When the block is firm enough to cut into cubes, the *paneer* is ready for use.

To make *chenna*, remove the cheese from the bag and knead the *paneer* well with the palms of your hands until it is very smooth. Combine the *paneer* with the sugar and maida, kneading in the sugar until it is fully incorporated.

YOGHURT

600 ml (2½ cups) milk
2 tablespoons thick plain yoghurt

Makes 600 ml (2½ cups)

Bring the milk to the boil in a heavy-based saucepan, then allow to cool to lukewarm. Stir in the yoghurt, cover and leave in a warm place for about 8 hours, or overnight. The yoghurt should be thick. If it is too runny, the milk was probably too hot for the starter yoghurt; if it is too milky, the yoghurt was probably not left in a warm enough place to ferment. From each batch, use 2 tablespoons to make the next batch.

When the yoghurt is set, put it in a sieve lined with a piece of muslin and leave to drain overnight. This will give a thick yoghurt that does not contain too much moisture.

TAMARIND PUREE

150 g (6 oz) tamarind block,
broken into small pieces

Makes 300 ml (1¼ cups)

Put the tamarind in a bowl, pour in 250 ml (1 cup) very hot water and soak for 3 hours or until the tamarind is soft. (If you are in a hurry, simmer the tamarind in the water for 15 minutes. Although this is efficient, it doesn't give as good a result.) Mash the tamarind thoroughly with a fork.

Strain the mixture through a sieve and extract as much of the pulp as possible by pushing it against the sieve with the back of a spoon. Put the tamarind mixture into the bowl with another 100 ml (½ cup) hot water and mash again. Strain again. Discard the fibres left in the sieve. The purée can be frozen in 1 tablespoon portions and defrosted as needed.

GARAM MASALA

8 cardamom pods
2 Indian bay leaves (cassia leaves)
1 teaspoon black peppercorns
2 teaspoons cumin seeds
2 teaspoons coriander seeds
5 cm (2 in) piece of cinnamon stick
1 teaspoon cloves

Makes 3 tablespoons

Remove the seeds from the cardamom pods. Break the bay leaves into small pieces. Put the seeds and bay leaves and remaining spices in a spice grinder or use a mortar and pestle to grind to a fine powder. Store in a small airtight container until needed.

CHAAT MASALA

4 tablespoons coriander seeds
2 tablespoons cumin seeds
1 teaspoon ajowan
3 tablespoons black salt
1 tablespoon amchoor powder
2 dried chillies
1 teaspoon black peppercorns
1 teaspoon pomegranate seeds

Makes 10 tablespoons

Place a small frying pan over low heat and dry-roast the coriander seeds until aromatic. Remove from the pan and dry-roast the cumin seeds then, separately, the *ajowan*. Grind the roasted mixture to a fine powder with the other ingredients, using a spice grinder or mortar and pestle. Store in an airtight container.

glossary

ajowan (ajwain) This spice resembles miniature cumin seeds and has a similar aroma but stronger flavour. Use sparingly.

amchoor/amchur powder *(khatai)* A beige powder made from dried green mangoes. It is used as a souring agent or meat tenderizer in Indian cooking.

asafoetida (hing) This pungent flavouring is the dried latex of a type of fennel. Its powerful aroma complements lentils, vegetables and pickles. Use sparingly. Available from Indian food shops.

atta Also known as chapati flour, this flour is made from ground durum wheat. It is used for making unleavened breads.

besan flour Also known as gram flour, this flour is made from ground chickpeas. It is used as a thickener in curries, and in batters, dumplings, sweets and breads.

black salt *(kala namak)* A rock salt with a tangy, smoky flavour. Available as black or dark brown lumps, or ground to a grey powder. Buy at Indian food shops.

chaat masala Seasoning used for snacks known as *chaat.* It comprises a variety of flavourings such as asafoetida, cumin, *amchoor,* black salt, cayenne, *ajowan* and pepper. (See page 251.)

chana dal (gram lentils) These are husked, split, polished, yellow gram. They are often cooked with a pinch of asafoetida to make them easier to digest.

chenna Sweetened Indian cheese, used in sweet dishes. Found in the refrigerated section in supermarkets and Indian food shops. (See page 249.)

curry leaves *(kadhi patta/meetha neem)* Smallish green aromatic leaves of a tree native to India and Sri Lanka. They are usually fried and added to the dish or used as a garnish at the end.

dal (dhal) is used to describe not only an ingredient but a dish made from it. In India, dal relates to any type of dried split pea, bean or lentil. The cooking times vary as do the texture and flavour. A dal dish can be a thin soup or a stew.

degchi A tinned-brass cooking pot with straight sides and no handles.

drumsticks *(sahjan)* Long, dark green, ridged fibrous pods from the horseradish tree. The inner pulp is the only part eaten. Available from Indian food shops.

fenugreek *(methi)* **seeds** Not a true seed, but a dried legume. Ochre in colour and almost square, with a groove down one side, fenugreek has a curry aroma and is best dry-roasted for a few seconds before use. Don't brown them too much or they will be bitter.

garam masala A northern Indian spice mix containing coriander, cumin, cloves, cardamom, black pepper, cinnamon and nutmeg. It is added to meat dishes as a final seasoning. (See page 251.)

ghee A highly clarified butter made from cow or water buffalo milk. Ghee can be heated to a high temperature without burning and has an aromatic flavour. Vegetable ghees are also available but don't have the same aromatic qualities. You can substitute clarified butter, or make your own ghee by melting unsalted butter in a saucepan, bringing to a simmer and cooking for about 30 minutes to evaporate out any water. Skim any scum from the surface, then drain off the ghee, leaving the white sediment behind. Leave to cool.

Indian bay leaves *(tej patta)* These are the dried leaves of the cassia tree. They look like dried European bay leaves but they have a cinnamon flavour. They are available from Indian food shops.

jaggery *(gur)* Made from sugar cane, this is a raw sugar with a caramel flavour and alcoholic aroma. Sold in lumps, it is sticky and varies in colour, depending on the juice from which it is made. Jaggery can also refer to palm sugar. Soft brown sugar can be used as a substitute.

kalonji (nigella seeds) Small black seeds with an onion flavour, used both as a spice in northern India and as a decoration for breads such as *naan*.

karhai/kadhai A deep wok-shaped cooking dish. Heavy cast-iron *karhais* are best for *talawa* (deep-frying) and carbon steel ones for *bhoona* (frying).

kokum The dried purple fruit of the gamboge tree which is used to impart an acid fruity flavour. Kokum looks like dried pieces of purple-black rind and is quite sticky. It needs to be briefly soaked before use. Kokum is available from Indian food shops as is the smoked version known as *kodampodli*.

maida Plain white flour used for making *naan* (bread) and other Indian recipes. Plain flour is a suitable substitute.

masoor dal (red lentils) When whole (known as *matki* or *bagali*), these are dark brown or green. When split, they are salmon in colour. The split ones are the most common as they cook more easily and do not usually need soaking as the whole ones do.

moong dal These are split and skinned mung beans. This pale yellow dal does not always need to be soaked. Whole mung beans *(sabat moong)*, also called green gram, must be soaked before use.

paneer A fresh cheese made by coagulating milk with lemon juice and leaving it to drain. Paneer is usually pressed into a block and can be found in the refrigerated section in supermarkets and Indian food shops. (See page 249.)

pomegranate seeds *(anardana)* These can be sun-dried whole or ground and are used to add a sour, tangy flavour to north Indian dishes. They are also used as a garnish. Buy at Indian food shops.

puffed rice *(moori, mamra, kurmura)* Similar to popcorn, puffed rice is made by exploding dried rice out of its husks by dropping the grains onto hot sand. It is used in snacks such as *bhel puri*, or rolled in jaggery to make sweets. Available from Indian food shops.

rice sticks (rice vermicelli, *chaaval ke sev*) Made from rice flour, these noodles are very thin. They are used for sweets or savoury snacks and need to be softened in boiling water.

sabat urad (whole black gram/black lentils) This whole *urad dal* has a black skin. Usually it has to be soaked or precooked before use. It gives a nutty taste and chewy texture to a dish.

sev Very fine noodles, used in *bhel puri*, made from besan flour. They are available from Indian food shops.

silver leaf *(varak)* Very thin, edible sheets of silver. They have no flavour or aroma and come in boxes or books between sheets of tissue paper. Always apply the silver to the food from the backing sheet

and then pull off the backing sheet. If you touch the foil it will stick to you. Silver leaf does not go on in an even layer because it is so fragile.

tamarind *(imli)* A souring agent made from the pods of the tamarind tree. Sold either as a block of pulp, fibrous husk and seeds, as cleaned pulp, or as ready-prepared tamarind purée or concentrate. (See page 250.)

tarka A seasoning process, either the first or last step, used in Indian cookery. Spices and aromatics are fried in oil to flavour the oil, then the oil is stirred into the dish, usually at the end of cooking.

tava A specially shaped hotplate used in India to cook breads. Some are flat, others are slightly convex or concave. Keep oiled to stop them going rusty. Non-stick ones are also available.

toor dal (toovar dal) Also called yellow lentils, toor dal is mostly eaten whole but can be puréed to make a pancake batter. Soak for a few hours before cooking.

urad dal (black lentils) The split variety *(chilke urad)* is a cream colour with black skin. The skinned variety is cream. Urad dal does not usually need to be soaked. The dal is used when making *dosa* and *idli* batters and it becomes glutinous and creamy when cooked.

yoghurt *(dahi, doi)* Yoghurt in India is made with whole milk and is quite thick. If you use commercial yoghurt, you may need to drain it in muslin first to remove any excess liquid. (See page 250.)

index

Published by Murdoch Books®, a division of Murdoch Magazines Pty. Ltd.
© Text, design, photography and illustrations Murdoch Books® 2003. All rights reserved. First published 2003.

Chief Executive: Juliet Rogers
Publisher: Kay Scarlett

Creative Director: Marylouise Brammer
Design Concept: Vivien Valk
Designer: Susanne Geppert
Food Editor: Lulu Grimes
Photographers: Jason Lowe (location); Alan Benson (recipes)
Stylist: Sarah de Nardi
Stylist's Assistants: Rekha Arnott, Sonia Grieg, Julie Ray
Recipes: Priya Wickramasinghe, Carol Selva Rajah
Additional Recipes: Kuvel Sundar Singh, Lisa Harvey, Margaret Grimes,
Ajoy Joshi, Rekha Arnott, Radha Jayaram
Additional Text: Kay Halsey

Editorial Director: Diana Hill
Editor: Carla Holt
Production: Fiona Byrne

National Library of Australia Cataloguing-in-Publication Data
A little taste of India. Includes index.
ISBN 1 74045 213 5.
1. Cookery, Indian. 641.5954

PRINTED IN CHINA by Leefung-Asco
No part of this publication may be reproduced, stored in a retrieval system or transmitted in any form or by
any means, electronic, mechanical, photocopying, recording or otherwise without the prior written permission
of the publisher. Murdoch Books® is a subsidiary of Murdoch Magazines Australia Pty Ltd.

Murdoch Books® Australia
GPO Box 1203, Sydney, NSW 2001
Phone: 61 (0) 2 4352 7000   Fax: 61 (0) 2 4352 7026

Murdoch Books UK Ltd
Ferry House, 51–57 Lacy Road,
Putney, London SW15 1PR
Phone: + 44 (0) 20 8355 1480
Fax: + 44 (0) 20 8355 1499

IMPORTANT: Those who might be at risk from the effects of salmonella food poisoning (the elderly,
pregnant women, young children and those suffering from immune deficiency diseases) should
consult their GP with any concerns about eating raw eggs.